Essential Maths

4

Jayashri Bhattacharya

Preface

Mathematics has always been an integral part of human life. From times immemorial, Mathematics has been in our everyday life in various ways irrespective of our knowledge of the mathematical concepts involved in various activities. The school curriculum focuses on the mathematical concepts to cultivate thinking and developing the reasoning skills. It enables the students to take up a systematic approach to solve their daily life problems, aims at exploring multiple aspects of the subject and thus develop a passion for it.

Essential Maths is a series that strives to focus on the maximum involvement of children following an interactive learning pattern. It has been authored by a senior teacher who has been dedicating her years to the teaching of this subject. Following this series will help students to keep away from rote learning and develop their confidence. Their increased confidence and flexibility with numbers will help them handle abstractions and develop logical approach towards the subject. The review exercises help the learners assess their understanding of the concepts. This series also develops the potential of the learners for continuous and comprehensive evaluation, by inculcating the scholastics and co-scholastic skills. Its activity based interactive style will sharpen the learners' minds and make learning enriching and joyous. The books are beautifully illustrated which adds to the overall appeal of the series.

From the Author

Mathematics has always been an integral part of human life. We use mathematics in our everyday life in various ways without being aware of our knowledge of the mathematical concepts involved in the activity. School curriculum includes the study of Mathematics in order to focus on mathematical concepts which help to cultivate the thinking and reasoning skills. It is a systematic approach to enable students to solve their daily life problems. It also aims to allow the students to explore the multiple aspects of the subject and develop a passion for it.

The lab activities and exercises can be used by the teachers as a demonstrative tool in the Maths Lab.

Objectives of teaching Mathematics are:

- To develop an ability to think and reason mathematically
- To handle abstractions
- To cultivate a positive attitude towards mathematics following an interactive learning pattern to help the teacher ensure maximum involvement of the learners
- To increase confidence and flexibility of the learners when numbers are concerned
- To discourage rote learning
- To develop logical sense along with a passion for the subject

The series **Essential Maths** is a carefully graded series prepared in accordance with the new syllabus prescribed by the NCERT on the basis of CCE (Continuous and Comprehensive Evaluation). A remarkable feature of this series is that all the exercises are formed in such a manner that they begin with easy exercises and gradually progresses to difficult ones. The books are activity based and extensive drilling with integrated revision exercises form its key feature. All the books are full of colourful illustrations which make learning a joy! They also inculcate scholastic and co-scholastic skills in the learner.

I take this opportunity to thank a few people who have helped me write this series. They are Ms Seema Chawla my editor for continuously guiding me, my friend Ms Tapasi (Managing Editor, B Jain), my parents-in-law for encouraging me and Aurobindo, my husband, for being very supportive. Heartfelt thanks to Sofia and Shantanu, my kids. Without their suggestions and criticism, I would not have been able to undertake and complete this project.

Jayashri Bhattacharya

Contents

Revision

1

1. Write the number names for the following numbers.

a. 4340

b. 7019

c. 8598

d. 6914

e. 3711

f. 5063

g. 2417

h. 1805

2. Write the number for the following names.

a. Three thousand four

b. Five thousand seventy seven

c. Five thousand eighty

d. Six thousand forty four

e. Eight thousand eight

f. Four thousand

g. One thousand two hundred thirty four

3. Write the number for the following

a. 8 thousands + 4 tens + 6 ones

b. 6 thousands + 3 ones

c. 4 thousands + 7 hundreds + 5 ones

d. 2 thousands + 9 hundreds + 3 tens + 8 ones

4. Write in the expanded form

a. 4340 ☐ + ☐ + ☐ + ☐

b. 7501 ☐ + ☐ + ☐ + ☐

c. 3040 ☐ + ☐ + ☐ + ☐

d. 1806 ☐ + ☐ + ☐ + ☐

e. 8749 ☐ + ☐ + ☐ + ☐

f. 6005 ☐ + ☐ + ☐ + ☐

5. Write the following numbers in ascending order.

a. 5684, 5864, 5486, 5468

b. 420, 3120, 5030, 6010

c. 7136, 7306, 7603, 7630

d. 192, 312, 98, 89

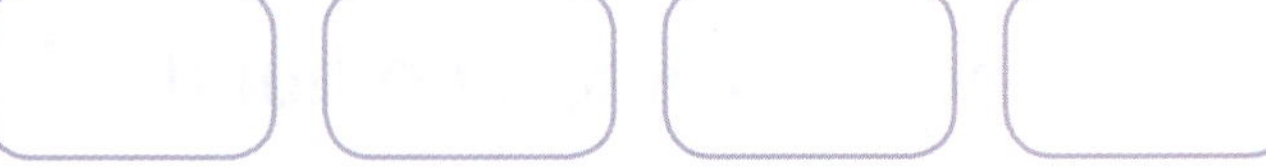

6. Write the following numbers in descending order.

a. 3081, 3881, 3801, 3108 ☐ ☐ ☐ ☐

b. 5555, 6666, 8888, 4444 ☐ ☐ ☐ ☐

c. 7465, 7605, 7504, 754 ☐ ☐ ☐ ☐

d. 6423, 3426, 4236, 2436 ☐ ☐ ☐ ☐

7. Fill in the boxes

a. Predecessor of the smallest 4-digit number is ☐

b. ☐ + 1 = Greatest 4-digit number

8. Add

a.
```
  587
 +346
 ____
 ____
```

b.
```
  636
  +98
 +247
 ____
 ____
```

c.
```
  3868
 +4757
 _____
 _____
```

d.
```
  7361
  +909
   +90
    +9
 _____
 _____
```

e.
```
  8017
  +566
  +132
   +85
 _____
 _____
```

f.
```
  1111
 +2222
 +3333
  +444
 _____
 _____
```

g.
```
  2060
  1707
 +3003
  +444
 _____
 _____
```

9. Subtract

a. $\begin{array}{r} 875 \\ -348 \\ \hline \end{array}$

b. $\begin{array}{r} 1900 \\ -642 \\ \hline \end{array}$

c. $\begin{array}{r} 4675 \\ -2989 \\ \hline \end{array}$

d. $\begin{array}{r} 7865 \\ -6875 \\ \hline \end{array}$

e. $\begin{array}{r} 8134 \\ -7968 \\ \hline \end{array}$

f. $\begin{array}{r} 1405 \\ -899 \\ \hline \end{array}$

g. $\begin{array}{r} 5079 \\ -3790 \\ \hline \end{array}$

h. $\begin{array}{r} 2222 \\ -1101 \\ \hline \end{array}$

10. Find the product

a. $\begin{array}{r} 338 \\ \times 4 \\ \hline \end{array}$

b. $\begin{array}{r} 28 \\ \times 54 \\ \hline \end{array}$

c. $\begin{array}{r} 74 \\ \times 47 \\ \hline \end{array}$

d. $\begin{array}{r} 303 \\ \times 55 \\ \hline \end{array}$

e. $\begin{array}{r} 295 \\ \times 44 \\ \hline \end{array}$

f. $\begin{array}{r} 427 \\ \times 17 \\ \hline \end{array}$

g. $\begin{array}{r} 430 \\ \times 30 \\ \hline \end{array}$

h. $\begin{array}{r} 111 \\ \times 33 \\ \hline \end{array}$

11. Divide

a. $4\overline{)480}$

b. $8\overline{)568}$

c. $9\overline{)296}$

d. $7\overline{)784}$

e. $5\overline{)311}$

f. $6\overline{)724}$

g. $5\overline{)905}$

h. $4\overline{)752}$

12. Convert as directed

a. 24 rupees 50 paise into paise = ______________p

b. 3 l to ml = ______________ ml

c. 7035p into ₹ and paise = ₹______________

d. 12 km to metres = ______________ m

e. 300 minutes to hours = ______________ hours

f. 7 km 200 m to metres = ______________ metres

g. 4 hours to minutes = ______________ mins

h. 5000 ml to litres = ______________ l

i. 6000 m to kilometres = ______________ km

j. 240 minutes to hours = ______________hrs

13. Shade the figure according to the fraction given.

a. $\frac{2}{3}$

b. $\frac{3}{4}$ 

c. $\frac{1}{4}$

d. $\frac{1}{3}$ 

14. Read the clock and write the time in two ways.

a.

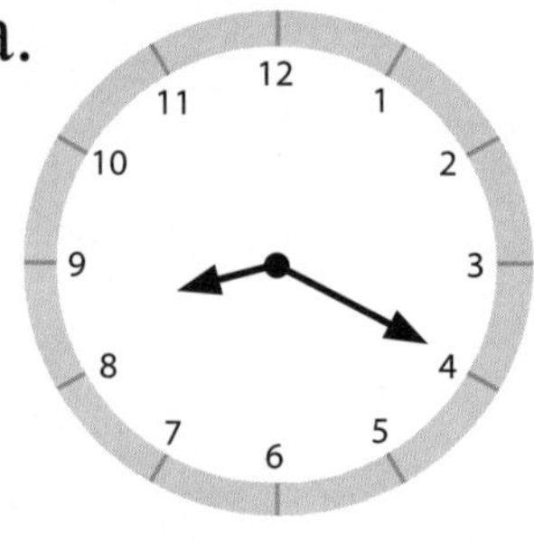

____

____

b.

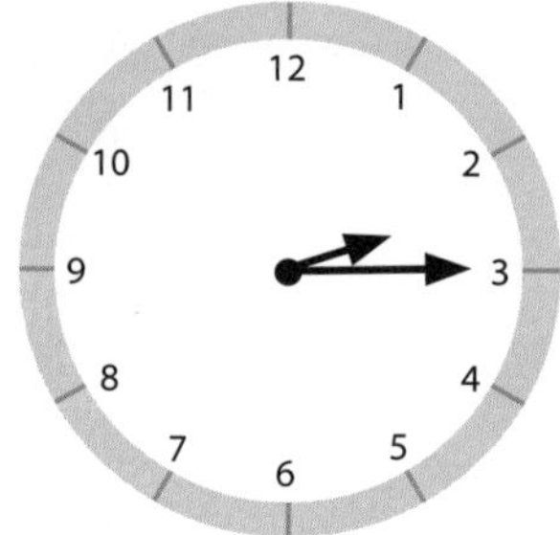

____

____

Large Numbers

2

We studied numbers from 1 to 9999

Greatest 1-digit number 9 + 1 = 10 [smallest 2-digit number]

Greatest 2-digit number 99 + 1 = 100 [smallest 3-digit number]

Greatest 3-digit number 999 + 1 = 1000 [smallest 4-digit number]

Greatest 4-digit number 9999 + 1 = 10000 [smallest 5-digit number]

10000 is read as ten thousand

The Periods

To make it easy to read and write large numbers, the place value chart has been divided into periods

Place value chart

Periods	Lakhs		Thousands		Ones		
Places	TL	L	T Th	Th	H	T	O
	Ten Lakhs	Lakh	Ten Thousand	Thousand	Hundred	Tens	Ones

The ones period consists of ones, tens, hundreds (3 Places)

The thousands period consists of thousands and ten thousands (2 Places)

The lakhs period consists of lakhs & ten lakhs (2 Places)

To show periods commas are used

EXAMPLE

A numeral of 5-digit is written like this

	T	L	T Th	Th	H	T	O	Number name
1.	65432		6	5	4	3	2	Sixty five thousand four hundred thirty two
2.	146029	1,	4	6,	0	2	9	One lakh forty six thousand and twenty nine
3.	56100	5,	6	1,	0	0	0	Five lakh sixty one thousand

EXAMPLE

On Abacus

69701

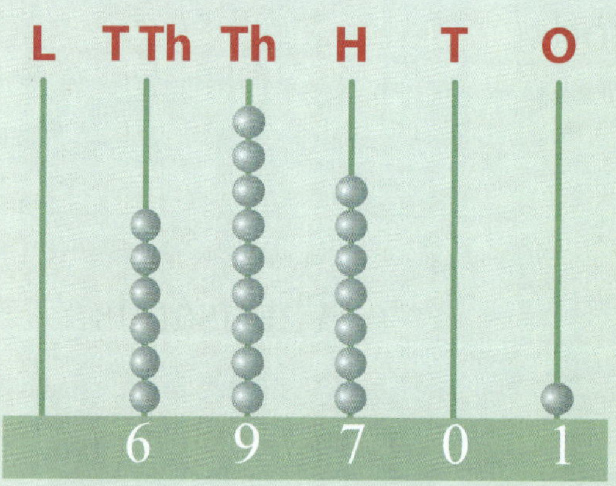

Exercise 2.1

1. Showing numbers on abacus, write the number names.

a.	36009	e.	1000004
b.	1000001	f.	700259
c.	72836	g.	2022022
d.	60606	h.	430043

2. Write the numeral for the number name using commas for periods.

a. Three lakhs twenty six ______________

b. Two lakhs seven hundred ______________

c. Five lakh thirty ______________

d. Eight lakhs eight thousand four hundred ______________

e. Ninety four thousand ninety ______________

3. Understand the pattern and complete the series.

a. 67,200; 68,200; __________; __________; __________;

b. 3,02,304; 3,02,404; __________; __________; __________;

c. 4,56,789; 5,56,789; __________; __________; __________;

Place Value

The place value of a digit in a numeral is according to the place it is in. If we have a numeral like 236879, we first put it in a place value chart, like this

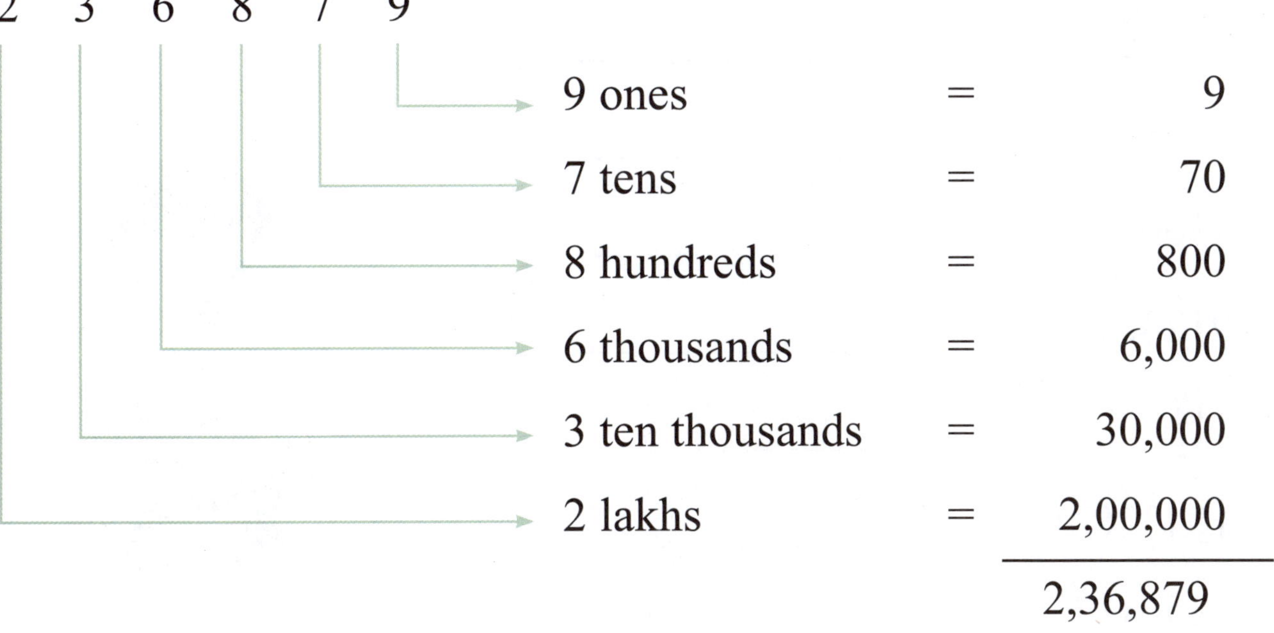

Expanded Form

Let us take the numeral 214687

L TTh Th H T O

2, 1 4, 6 8 7 = 2 lakhs + 1 ten thousand + 4 thousands+ 6 hundreds + 8 tens + 7 ones

2,14,687 can he written in 2 other ways

$2{,}14{,}687 = 2 \times 1{,}00{,}000 + 1 \times 10{,}000 + 4 \times 1000 + 6 \times 100 + 8 \times 10 + 7 \times 1$

$2{,}14{,}687 = 2{,}00{,}000 + 10{,}000 + 4{,}000 + 600 + 80 + 7$

Exercise 2.2

1. Write the place value of the underlined digits in the following numerals.

   a. $9\underline{6}325$ ____________________

   b. $4446\underline{6}$ ____________________

   c. $150\underline{8}73$ ____________________

   d. $4\underline{3}0003$ ____________________

   e. $\underline{9}12307$ ____________________

   f. $11\underline{1}111$ ____________________

   g. $1\underline{0}4320$ ____________________

   h. $8430\underline{1}$ ____________________

2. Fill in the blanks.

a. 86534 = ☐ Ten thousands + ☐ Thousands + ☐ Hundreds + ☐ Tens + ☐ Ones

b. 376251 = ☐ × 1,00,000 +7 × ☐ + ☐ × 1000 + 2 × ☐ + 5 × ☐ + ☐

c. 5,29,540 = 5,00,000 + ☐ + ☐ + ☐ + ☐ + ☐

3. Write in the expanded form.

a. 37018 ☐

b. 4297816 ☐

c. 806001 ☐

d. 2000040 ☐

e. 406308 ☐

f. 550403 ☐

4. Write the short form for

a. 700000 + 8000 + 700 + 7 ☐

b. 8 thousands + 8 tens ☐

c. 30000 + 30 + 3 ☐

d. 5000 + 600 + 20 + 7 ☐

e. 7 × 100000 + 2 × 10000 + 6 × 1000 + 4 × 100 + 8 × 10 ☐

Ordering of Numbers

When 2 numbers have to be **compared** we count the number of digits

The number with greater number of digits is greater

If they have the same number of digits, We observe the value of the periods of the two numbers

EXAMPLE

1. Compare 72428 and 53989

Solution:

TTh	Th	H	T	O
7	2	4	2	8
5	3	9	8	9

Consider the digits in ten thousands place

7 ten thousands > 5 ten thousands

$\therefore$ 72,428 > 53,989

EXAMPLE

2. Compare 48315 and 48513

Solution:

TTh	Th	H	T	O
4	8	3	1	5
4	8	5	1	3

compare the digits in ten thousands place. They are same. The digits in thousands place are also same.

So, we campare the digits in the hundred's place.

3 hundreds < 5 hundreds

$\therefore$ 48,315 < 48,513

3. Arrange 54378, 54630; 61121 in ascending order.

Solution: Put these numbers in the place value chart.

TTh	Th	H	T	O
5	4	3	7	8
5	4	6	3	0
6	1	1	2	1

6 ten thousands > 5 ten thousands

6 hundreds > 3 hundreds So, 61121 is greatest and 54378 is smallest

the order is 61,121 > 54,630 > 54,378

Exercise 2.3

1. Fill in the circle with the correct sign (>, <, =).

a. 690148 ◯ 690184

b. 35439 ◯ 3539

c. 40040 ◯ 40004

d. 356985 ◯ 356895

e. 34296 ◯ 34293

f. 210210 ◯ 201020

g. 110110 ◯ 22022

h. 18348 ◯ 18344

2. Write in the ascending order.

a. 20648, 19670, 54187, 65771

b. 396452, 209586, 814792, 278934

c. 168390, 284570, 268750, 278934

3. Write in the descending order.

a. 548275, 584725, 569875, 598175 [ ] [ ] [ ] [ ]

b. 25269, 25629, 25962, 25296 [ ] [ ] [ ] [ ]

c. 228696, 28962, 282669, 228966 [ ] [ ] [ ] [ ]

Successor and Predecessor

The successor of a number is 1 more than the number

Successor = Number+1

The predecessor of a number is 1 less than the number

Predecessor = Number -1

Greatest and smallest numbers using given digits.

- To write the largest number we write the digits in descending order.
- To write the smallest number we write the digits in ascending order. 'O' is never the first digit.

EXAMPLE

Make the largest and smallest number using the digits 4, 2, 1, 8, 9 only once.

Solution : Largest number is 9 8 4 2 1

Smallest number is 1 2 4 8 9

Exercise 2.4

1. Find the greatest and the smallest numbers using the following digits.

	Greatest	Smallest
a. 2, 8, 5, 6, 0,1		
b. 7, 0, 9, 8,6		
c. 8, 9, 6, 5, 0, 1		
d. 6, 5, 4, 0, 2, 1		
e. 4, 0, 2, 8, 7, 1		

2. Write the predecessor of:

a. ______ 570199

b. ______ 100010

c. ______ 439100

d. ______ 679999

e. ______ 934100

3. Write the successor of:

a. 610000 ______

b. 900909 ______

c. 301006 ______

d. 273459 ______

e. 27403 ______

4. Write the successor of the greatest 5-digit number. Write its number name also.
5. Write the predecessor of the smallest 6-digit number. Write its number name also.

Indian System of Numeration

We in India use Indian system of numeration

Indian Place Value Chart

Periods	LAKHS	THOUSANDS	ONES
	TL L	T Th Th	H T O

ONES period has 3-digits

THOUSANDS period has 2-digits

LAKHS period has 2-digits

International System

Outside India International System is used. They do not understand lakhs or crores, like in India we do not understand millions, which is used in international system.

Number	Millions			Thousands			Ones		
	Hundred Millions	Ten Millions	Millions	Hundred Thousands	Ten Thousands	Thousands	Hundreds	Tens	Ones
38425976		3	8	4	2	5	9	7	6
803040572	8	0	3	0	4	0	5	2	2

In the International system every period has 3-digits

EXAMPLE

Write the number in International system and write the number name
634856

Hth	TTh	Th	H	T	O
6	3	4,	8	5	6

six hundred thirty four thousand and eight hundred and fifty six

Exercise 2.5

1. Rewrite with commas

	Number	Indian System	International System
a.	185602		
b.	300246		
c.	4281510		
d.	5000000		
e.	215746		

2. Mark the periods and write number names using the Indian System.

   a. 707770 b. 100001 c. 304528 d. 97315

3. Mark the periods and write number names using International System.

   a. 123432 b. 600660 c. 380764 d. 5000000 e. 400004

4. Write the numerals for the following.

   a. Three lakhs one thousand twenty
   b. Forty seven lakh forty seven thousand forty seven
   c. Three hundred four thousand three hundred six
   d. Five million two hundred six thousand eighty
   e. Ninety thousand ninety

Rounding Numbers— Estimation

Harry went to a birthday party. When he came back, his father asked him, "How was the party?" Harry said, "Great! Many of my friends were there and we enjoyed!"

His father asked, "How many of your friends were there?" Harry said, "I did not count. I don't know."

"You surely can guess. Roughly 10 or 20," he said. Harry hesitated and said, "Around 20."

Next day, Harry asked his friend and came to know there were 22 including Harry. So, there are situations where we round a number to a convenient figure.

How many people in the city? Around 6 lakhs.

How many passengers in the train? About 1200.

EXAMPLE

Example 1: I have 42 toffees. I say, 'I have about 40 toffees.' (I rounded to the nearest 10)

Example 2: Rahul had 88 marbles. He said, 'I have about 90 marbles.'

Example 3: Delhi to Mussore is 587 km. It is about 600 km (rounded to nearest hundred)

Rules

To the nearest ten

If it is 12, we round it to 10

If it is 416, we round it to 420

If it is 7133, we round it to 7130

If it is 6437, we round it to 6440

Step 1: Mark the periods

Step 2: Identify the place to be rounded off like the ones, in this case.

Step 3: If in ones place the digit is less than 5, the digit in tens place remains the same.

Step 4: If the digit in ones place is 5 or greater, the digit in tens place is rounded off to the next digit.

Number		Rounded to tens	Number		Rounded to tens
	O			O	
1	4	10	9	5	100
1	9	20	32	1	320
3	1	30	74	7	750
7	4	70	86	1	860
8	6	90	124	3	1240
3	7	40	257	9	2580
14	5	150	53	5	540

Rounded to the nearest 100

Step 1: Mark the periods and places

Step 2: Identify the place to be rounded off

Step 3: Check the digits to the right of the place to be rounded off.

If number in the tens and ones place is less than 50, the digits in the ones and the tens places become zero.

EXAMPLE

148 ⟶ $48 < 50$, 148 rounded to 100

158 ⟶ $58 > 50$, 158 rounded to 200.

so, 6219 is

6 2 19 ⟶ $19 < 50$ rounded to 6200

6287 ⟶ $87 > 50$, so 6287 is rounded to 6300

If the number in the tens and ones place is 50 or greater, the hundreds place digit is increased by I. When rounded the digits in the ones and tens places become zero

EXAMPLE **Round off the numbers to nearest 100.**

151 ⟶ $51 > 50$, Rounded to 200

374 ⟶ $74 > 50$, Rounded to 400

⟶ 1700

Exercise 2.6

1. Round off the following numbers to the nearest 10

a. 65	c. 179	e. 2482
b. 36968	d. 70986	f. 1998

2. Round off to the nearest 100

a. 26462	c. 384335	e. 849639
b. 78650	d. 477899	f. 555550

Rounding off to the nearest 1000

Step1: Mark the periods and place

Step2: Underline the place to be rounded off (thousands)

Step3: Check the number formed by the digits to the right of the underlined digit. If it is less than 500 the digit in thousands place does not change.

Step 4: If the number formed by the digits is greater than 500, the number is rounded off to the next thousand.

EXAMPLE

Round 61752 to the nearest thousand.

Solution :

TTh	Th	H	T	O
6	$\underline{1}$	7	5	2

The number formed by digits to the right of 1 is 752.

752 > 500

so, 61752 is rounded to 62, 000

Exercise 2.7

1. Round off the following numbers to the nearest 1000

   a. 36501 b. 154489

   c. 46701 d. 11111

   e. 55500

Roman Numerals

We studied the symbols used by Romans to represent numbers.

Roman	I	V	X	L	C	D	M
Hindu Arabic	1	5	10	50	100	500	1000

Ancient Romans did not use any symbol for digit 0.

Rules for forming Roman Numbers

If a symbol is placed **after** one of bigger value, it is **added** to the symbol.

VI = 5+1 = 6

XI = 10+1 =11

XXI = 10+10+1 =21

If a symbol is placed BEFORE a bigger value, it is subtracted

IV = 5 – 1 = 4

IX = 10 – 1 = 9

Rules

- No symbol can be repeated more than THREE times.
- V cannot be repeated
- I can be subtracted from V and X only
- When a smaller value is written between two symbols of greater value. It is subtracted from the greater numeral following it.

EXAMPLE

XIV = 10 + (5-1) = 14

CXXIV = 100+10+10+ (5-1) = 124

- Symbol X can be subtracted from L and C.

XL = 50-10 = 40

XC = 100-10 = 90

- V, L, D can never be subtracted.

EXAMPLE

Write in Roman numerals

39 = 30 + 9 = XXXIX

76 = 70 + 6 = LXXVI

69 = 60 + 9 = LXIX

EXAMPLE

Write in Hindu Arabic numeral

LXXIX = L + XX + IX

= 50 + 20 + 9

XLIII = XL + III

= 40 + 3 = 43

Exercise 2.8

1. Complete the table by filling in Hindu Arabic or Roman numerals.

a.

19	26		34	39		44	49	54				84	89
		XXIX			XL				LIX	I	LXXI		

b.

61	83		65	46	73		
		LXVI				XXIX	XXXVIII

2. The place value of the digits have to be put in order to find the numeral

   a. 7 + 800000 + 60 + 100 + 8000 ____________________

   b. 4000 + 100000 + 70 + 5200 ____________________

3. A teacher asked her student to write six lakhs five thousand four hundred and five. He writes 65205. Is he correct? If not, write the correct number.

4. Identify as given below and colour the creature

   a. The greatest 3-digit number (red)

   b. Smallest 5-digit number (pink)

c. Sum of smallest 2-digit number and greatest 3-digit number (green)

d. The greatest 4-digit number (blue)

e. Difference of greatest 2-digit number and smallest 3-digit number (yellow)

Lab Activity

Objective: Forming numbers

Materials required: Blank cards

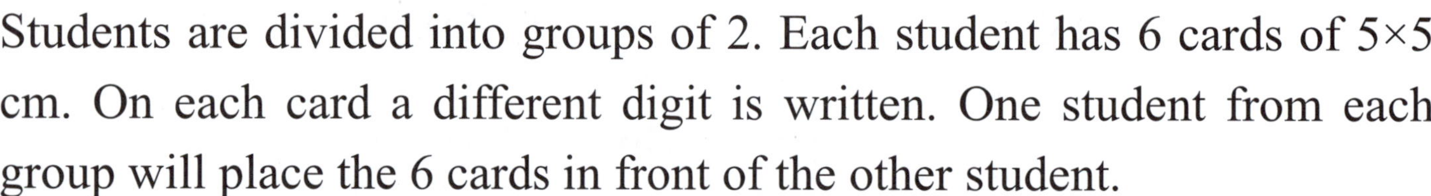

Students are divided into groups of 2. Each student has 6 cards of 5×5 cm. On each card a different digit is written. One student from each group will place the 6 cards in front of the other student.

The second student writes the numeral and the number name in Indian and International system.

The places can be changed and a new numeral and is formed the number names are written.

Whichever group campletes 6 numbers is the winner.

3	6	4	9	0	2

The teacher can ask the students to find the greatest and the smallest numbers formed, the place value of digits.

Speed and correctness is important

Mental Maths

1. Largest 5-digit number with two different digits is ________ (99998 / 99990).
2. Smallest 5-digit number with 3 different digits is ________ (10009 / 10002)
3. Smallest 5-digit number with all digits same is ________ (20000 / 11111)
4. Predecessor of one lakh is ________
5. Difference between the place values of the two 5 in 50,500 is ________.
6. 1 ten-thousand = ________ hundreds.

3

Addition

Addition of 5-digit or 6-digit numbers is just like addition of 4-digit numbers we learnt in class III

EXAMPLE

	TTh	Th	H	T	O
	1	3	4	5	6
+	2	4	3	2	0
	3	7	7	7	6

Step1: Arrange in columns according to place value

Step 2: Add ones

Step 3: Add tens

Step 4: Add hundreds

Step 5: Add thousands

Step 6: Add ten thousands

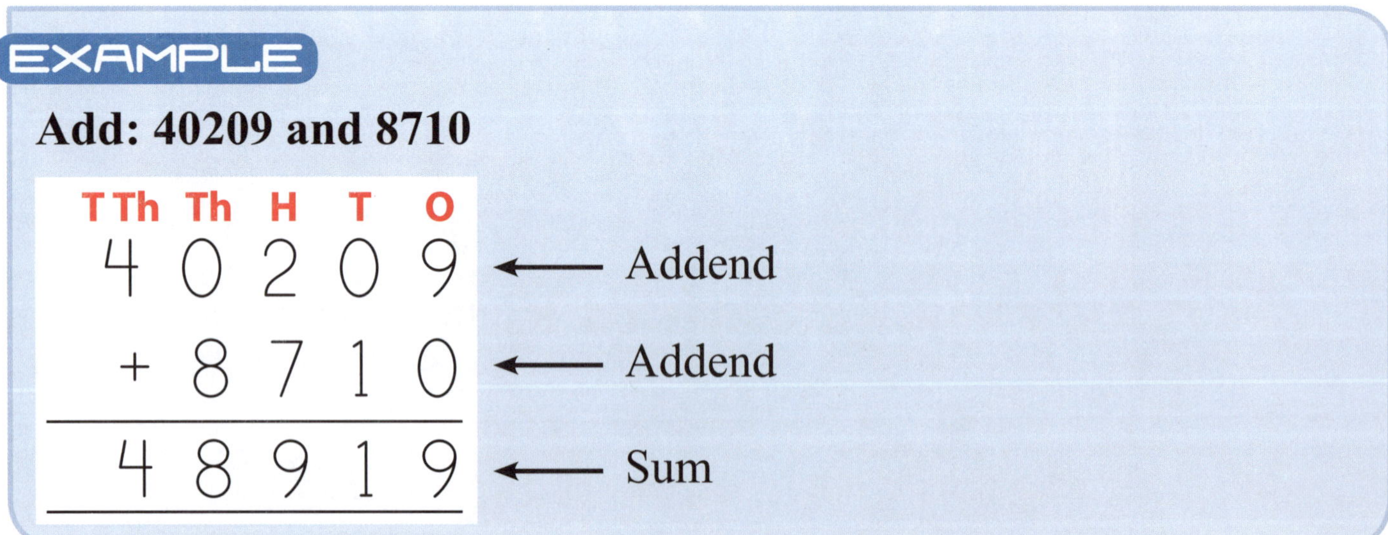

Addition with Regrouping

EXAMPLE

Add 23546 and 47658

	TTh	Th	H	T	O
	(1) 2	(1) 3	(1) 5	(1) 4	6
+	4	7	6	5	8
	7	1	2	0	4

7 1 2 0 4 ⟵ Sum

The sum of two or more numbers does not depend on the order of the addends.

Properties of Addition

Order of addends

$$\begin{array}{r} 24371 \\ +\ 35897 \\ \hline 60268 \\ \hline \end{array} \longleftarrow \text{Sum} \longrightarrow \begin{array}{r} 35897 \\ +\ 24371 \\ \hline 60268 \\ \hline \end{array}$$

$$\begin{array}{r} 35280 \\ +1793 \\ +\ 89 \\ \hline 37162 \\ \hline \end{array} \qquad \begin{array}{r} 1793 \\ +\ 35280 \\ +\ 89 \\ \hline 37162 \\ \hline \end{array} \qquad \begin{array}{r} 89 \\ +1793 \\ +35280 \\ \hline 37162 \\ \hline \end{array}$$

Adding zero to a number

38,263 + 0 = 38263

7,89,144 + 0 = 7,89,144

[When 0 is added to a number the sum is the number itself]

Exercise 3.1

1. Fill in the blanks.
   a. 3489 + __________ = 3889
   b. __________ + 0 = 98001
   c. Successor of 342101 is __________
   d. 92 + 328 + 8 = __________

2. Add

a.
```
  313256
 +452201
  347162
 -------

 -------
```

b.
```
  600538
 +  29745
 +   3897
 -------

 -------
```

c.
```
  425783
  367629
 + 25789
 -------

 -------
```

d.
```
   19280
 +  4089
 + 37089
 -------

 -------
```

e.
```
  326532
 + 32166
 +320632
 -------

 -------
```

f.
```
   64998
 +216324
 + 15516
 -------

 -------
```

g.

	6785
+	49817
+	155089

h.

	435363
+	262626
+	1717

i.

	5468
+	15454
+	254574

3. Addition

a. 6 thousands + 14 hundreds = 6th + 1th + 4h = ☐

b. 8 thousands+12 hundreds+18 tens (8th+1th+2h+1h+8t) = ☐

c. 6 ten thousands + 17 thousands = ☐

d. 2 thousands, 15 hundreds = ☐

e. 4 ten thousands + 16 thousands + 15 hundreds = ☐

4. Find the missing digits

a.

	3 ☐ 4 2 ☐
+	☐ 2 ☐ 3 1
	5 8 9 ☐ 6

b.

	4 6 ☐ 0 8
+	☐ 9 7 2 ☐
	6 ☐ 1 ☐ 5

c.

	☐ ☐ ☐ ☐ ☐
+	8 4 9 8 6
	1 2 2 6 4 3

d.

	5 4 ☐ 1 ☐
+	☐ 3 ☐ 3 2
	5 ☐ 6 4 6

e.

	4 6 ☐ 0 8
+	☐ 9 7 2 ☐
	6 ☐ 1 ☐ 5

f.

	3 4 2 6 8
+	☐ ☐ ☐ ☐ ☐
+	1 4 6 2
	6 3 0 7 3

5. Fill in the blanks

a. 38,476+ ____________ + 76,505 = ____________ + 18,409 + 38,476

b. 65,410 + 100 = ____________

c. 71,369 + 1 = ____________

d. 87,138 + 1,000 = ____________

e. 78,001 + ____________ = 78,001

f. 8,500 + ____________ = 9,000

Word Problems

EXAMPLE

A bag of toffees had 7893 chocolate toffees, 13650 coconut and 21264 orange flavour toffees. Find the total number of toffees.

No. of chocolate flavour toffees

No. of coconut flavour toffees

No. of orange flavour toffees

Total number of toffees in the bag is 42,807

	TTh	Th	H	T	O
		7	8	9	3
+	1	3	6	5	0
+	2	1	2	6	4
	4	2	8	0	7

Exercise 3.2

Solve the following problems

1. In a city there are 20849 men 18697 women and 25,932 children. What is the total population of the city?

+

Population

2. The number of tourists who visited Hong Kong in the month May were 1,20,387 and in June there were 95,654. How many people visited Hong Kong in these 2 months?

+

Population

3. The total number of students who appeared for class XII board exams from Meerut were 2,60,350 and from Panipat were 1,30,645. How many students appeared for the examination from these two places?

+

Students

4. A library has 1,25,400 books in English; 85,978 books in French, 10,659 books in German. Find the total number of books in the library

+

Books

5. A factory produced 46,517 LEDs in 2 months. If 38150 were produced in the 1st month, how many LEDs were produced in the second month?

−

Students

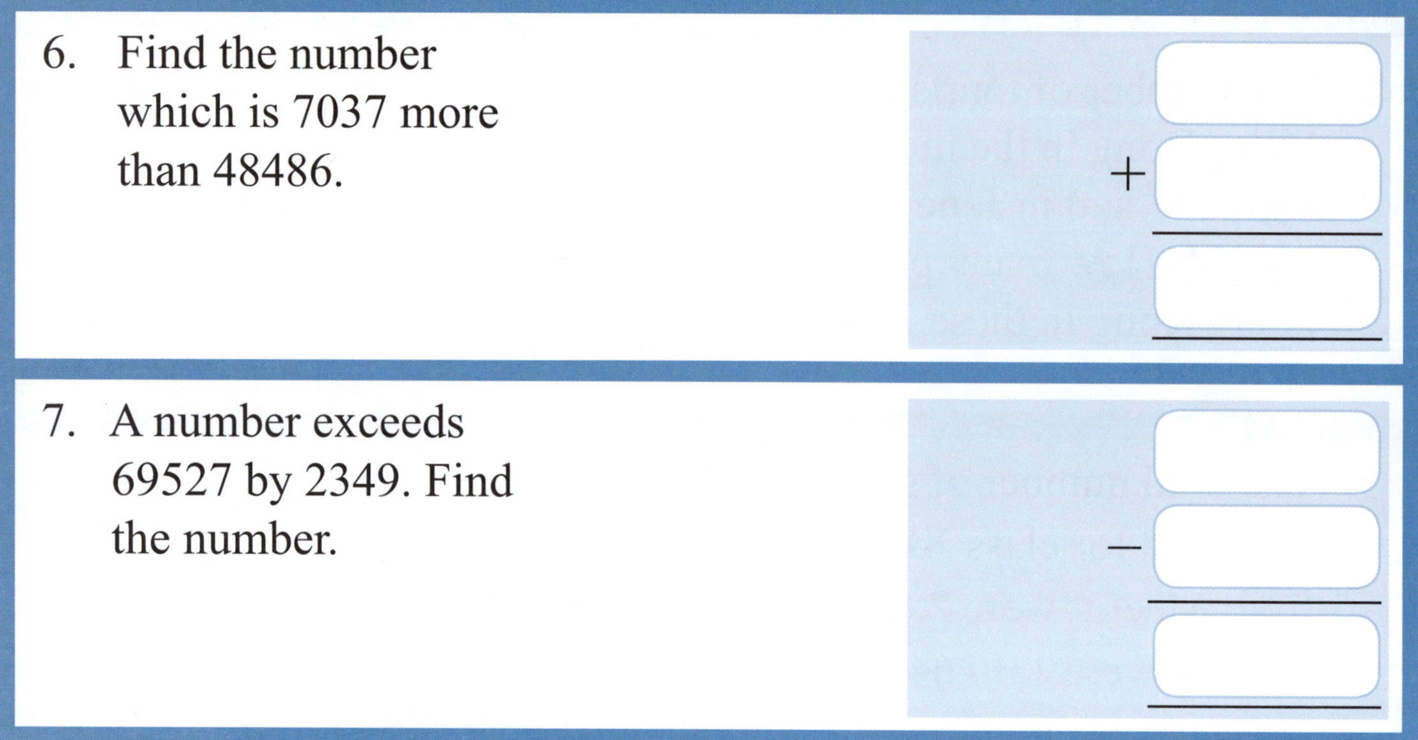

6. Find the number which is 7037 more than 48486.

7. A number exceeds 69527 by 2349. Find the number.

Estimating the sum

Medha's teacher gave her 2 numbers—3768 and 4925. She asked Medha to estimate the sum.

Medha rounded the 4-digit numbers to the nearest 1000 and immediately answered—4000 + 5000 = 9000

The teacher was very happy.

Remember

4-digit numbers are rounded to nearest thousand and 5-digit numbers are rounded to the nearest ten thousand

Exercise 3.3

1. Asha spent ₹ 1865 on shoes and ₹ 2490 on a dress. Estimate the total amount spent.
2. The distance from Delhi to Agra is 200 km and Agra to Jaipur is 230 km. Estimate the distance covered by Rahul if he went from Delhi to Agra to Jaipur by road. Also compare it with the actual distance covered.

3. Complete the table

S.no	Add	Rounding off	Estimated sum	Actual sum
a.	3412 + 7535	3000 + 8000	11000	10,947
b.	5639 + 1495			
c.	9833 + 29636			
d.	54545 + 45454			
e.	73196 + 29730			

Mental Maths

1. Fill in the missing digits.

a.

```
   4 3 2 □ 2
 + □ 2 □ 9 □
 -----------
   9 □ 4 3 9
```

2. Shyam's and Neha's ages add up to 20 years. What will their ages add up to after 5 years?
3. The number 100 more than 60,000 is ________.
4. 7,439 is ________ more than 6,439.
5. We add ________ to 4500 to make it 5000.
6. (9 + ________) + 8 = ________ + (11 + 8).
7. I was born in 2004. I will be 16 years old in ________.

Lab Activity

To understand the property of order of numbers that are added.

1. Divide the students into groups of 2.
2. Provide them with cards (blank)
3. Ask each group to write two 5-digit numbers on the cards.
4. They should be asked to find the sum of the two numbers.
5. Ask them to interchange the position of the cards and find the sum of the numbers.
6. Ask them to record the observation.

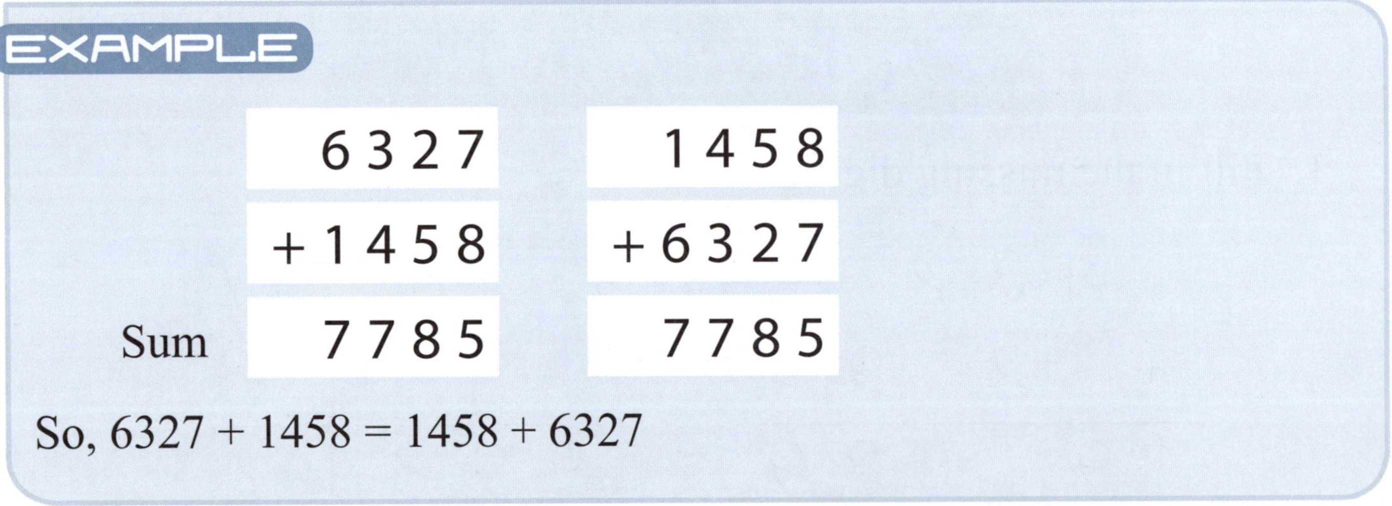

7. Students can be encouraged to try this for 6-digit numbers also.

Subtraction

4

Subtraction of 5-digit and 6-digit numbers are the same as subtraction of 4-digit numbers.

Subtraction without regrouping

EXAMPLE

Subtract 31204 form 67894

	TTh	Th	H	T	O
	6	7	8	9	4
−	3	1	2	0	4
	3	6	6	9	0

Step1: Write numbers in columns. Greater number is written above the smaller number.

Step 2: Subtract the ones

Step 3: Subtract the tens

Step 4: Subtract the hundred

Step 5: Subtract the thousands

Step 6: Subtract the ten thousands

Subtraction with regrouping

EXAMPLE

Subtract 13496 from 30170

	TTh	Th	H	T	O
	3	0	1	7	0
−	1	3	4	9	6
	1	6	6	7	4

Step 1: Write numbers in columns

Step 2: $0 < 6$. Change 1 ten to 10 ones. 6 Tens are left in tens column. 10 one- 6 ones = 4 ones

Step 3: Sub the tens $6 < 9$ change 1 H to 10 tens. 10 t + 6t = 16t
16t-9t = 7t
0H are left in Hundreds column

Step 4: 0 < 4 since we have O Th, change 1TTh = 10 Th
10Th – 1 Th = 9 TH in Th Column
2 T Th is left in T Th Column
Step 5: 10 H-4 H = 6 H
Step 6: 9 Th- 3 Th = 6 Th
Step 7: 2 T Th-1 T Th = 1T TH

Exercise 4.1

1. Subtract

a.
```
 64321
-53468
______
______
```

b.
```
 35817
-21999
______
______
```

c.
```
 46300
-39782
______
______
```

d.
```
735894
-98976
______
______
```

e.
```
 60303
-59786
______
______
```

f.
```
 200000
-117426
_______
_______
```

g.
```
 97245
-62187
______
______
```

h.
```
 75106
-58349
______
______
```

i.
```
 897000
-586357
_______
_______
```

2. Do as directed

   a. Subtract 23475 from the sum of 38700 and 19596.

   b. Subtract the sum of 12365 and 27958 from 100000.

   c. Find the number which is 2356 less than 10000.

   d. Subtract sixty five thousand four hundred and two from one lakh thirty.

   e. Subtract five lakh six thousand seven hundred and ninety from nine lakh thirty thousand.

3. Find the missing digits

a.
```
  7 5 4 □
-   □ □ □
---------
  5 4 6 2
```

b.
```
  □ □ □ □
- 3 2 7 6
---------
  6 7 8 9
```

c.
```
  2 4 3 □ 6
- □ 9 □ 5 □
-----------
  0 □ 1 4 6
```

d.
```
  7 6 0 4 3
- 4 □ 6 □ 2
-----------
  □ 6 □ 8 □
```

e.
```
  5 □ 2 □ 5
- □ 4 □ 8 □
-----------
  3 1 4 4 7
```

f.
```
  9 □ 4 □ 0
- 1 1 6 7 □
-----------
  0 □ 1 4 6
```

Exercise 4.2

Word Problems

1. The population of a town is 11,28,490. If 1,56,875 people left the town due to lack of some facilities, what is the town's population?

```
              1128490
           –   156875
           ----------
Population    □
```

2 Difference of two numbers is 46,135. If one of the numbers is 90,217, find the other number.

3. There were 6459 people in a train 2156 people got down in the first station and 1093 people got into the train. How many people were there in the train when it left the station?

People

4. On the first day of ticket sales of the Harry Potter movie 1,26,000 tickets were sold. On the second day 7355 less tickets were sold. How many tickets were sold on the second day?

Tickets

5. A man had ₹ 3 lakh. He gave ₹ 1 lakh and seventy five thousand to his brother; rupees ninety five thousand to his sister and the rest to his son. Find the amount his son got.

Amount

6. Cost of a Mercedes Benz car is ₹ 30,50,000. The cost of a Skoda car is ₹ 14,60,000 less than Mercedes. Find the cost of the Skoda car.

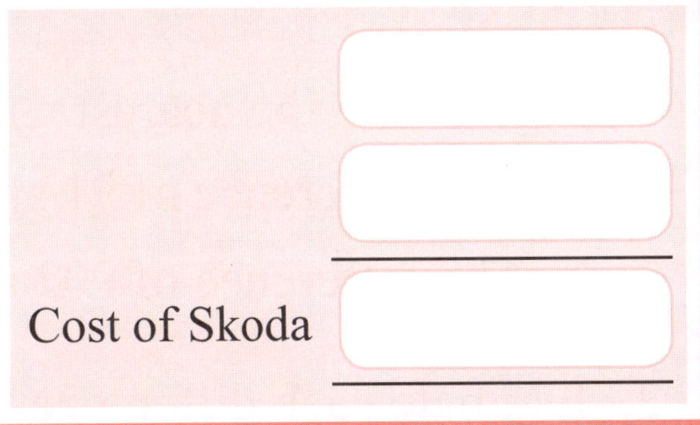

Estimating differences

Mr. Sinha goes to a showroom to buy a T.V. The T.V. he wants to buy is listed at ₹ 35,450. He was carrying ₹ 50,000 in cash. He wanted to estimate the money left with him after the purchase.

Many times we do not need the exact difference but just a round about idea of the difference. This is known as estimate.

Like for example,

EXAMPLE

Estimate 46240 – 32895 by rounding to the nearested thousands.

Solution: Rounding off to nearest thousands

46240 ⟶ 46000

32895 ⟶ – 33000

Estimate difference ⟶ 13000

EXAMPLE

Estimate 54816 – 25734 to nearest ten thousands

Solution: Rounding off to nearest ten thousands

54816 ⟶ 50,000

25734 ⟶ – 30,000

Estimate difference ⟶ 20,000

Exercise 4.3

1. Estimate to the nearest ten
   a. The difference of 91 and 45
   b. The difference of 902 and 204

2. Estimate each difference to the nearest hundred
   a. 706 and 278
   b. 3405 and 2376

3. Estimate to the nearest thousand
   a. 20512 – 4521 b. 7361 – 2806

4. A man earns ₹ 32,600 per month. If he saves ₹ 5,870 estimate the expenditure in that month.

Mental Maths

1. Fill in the missing digits.

a.

```
  2 □ 4 3 □
− □ 0 □ 6 8
-----------
  1 2 8 □ 3
-----------
```

b.

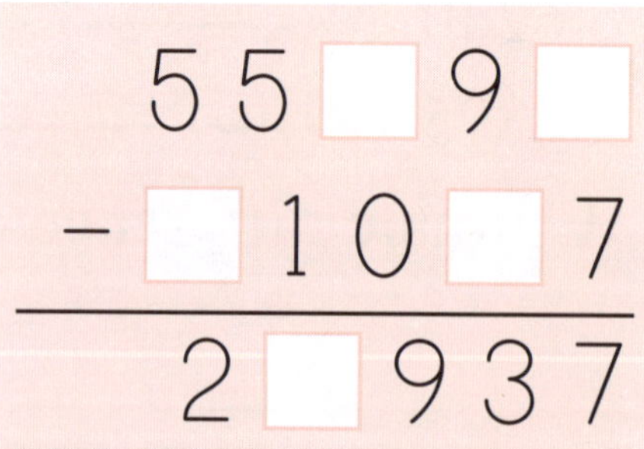

2. What is the difference between the greatest 6-digit number and 1 less than the smallest 7-digit number?

3. What is the difference between the greatest 5-digit number and the greatest 4-digit number?

Multiplication 5

The teacher asked Chinku and Cherry to count the number of children present in the class.

Cherry replied almost immediately, “39!” Chinku was still counting each head.

He asked. “Cherry, how did you do it so fast?”

She said, “Simple! There are 5 rows and 4 columns of benches and each bench has 2 students.”

$5 \times 4 \times 2 = 20 \times 2 \quad = 40 - 1$ (Suri is absent)

$= 39$

Cherry had used her knowledge of multiplication. So, if we have 5 baskets of 15 apples each.

The total number of apples is $15 + 15 + 15 + 15 + 15 = 75$

$15 \times 5 = 75$

Recapitulating properties of multiplication

$7 \times 1 = 7$

$298 \times 1 = 298$

$1035 \times 1 = 1035$

Product of a number and 1 is the number itself

9	×	5	=	45
5	×	9	=	45
20	×	4	=	80
4	×	20	=	80

Product of 2 numbers does not change even if the order of numbers to be multiplied, changes

(2×3)	×	4	=	6×4	=	24
2	×	(3×4)	=	2×12	=	24
10	×	20×40	=	10×800	=	8000
16	×	0	=	0		
789	×	0	=	0		

Product of any number and 0 is zero

Exercise 5.1

1. Fill in the blanks

   a. $726 \times$ ________ $= 7260$

   b. $2175 \times$ ________ $= 0$

   c. $97 \times 0 =$ ________

d. $648 \times$ _________ $= 237 \times 648$

e. $19 \times$ _________ $\times 78 =$ _________ $\times 46 \times 19$

f. $372 \times 30 =$ _________ $\times 372$

g. $1438 \times 61 \times$ _________ $= 0$

h. $9 \times$ _________ $= 108$

i. $8 \times 9 =$ _________

j. The _________ of 7×8 and 8×7 is the same.

Multiplication by 10, 100, 1000

$2 \times 10 = 20$

$25 \times 10 = 250$

$147 \times 10 = 1470$

When any number is multiplied by 10, put a zero at the right of the numeral.

$2 \times 100 = 1200$

$35 \times 100 = 3500$

$256 \times 100 = 25600$

When a number is multiplied by 100, add two zeroes after the numeral.

Multiplication by 20, 30, 200, 300, 2000, 9000

$2 \times 20 = 2 \times 2 \times 10 = 2 \times 2 \times 10 = 40$

$3 \times 200 = 3 \times 2 \times 100 = 6 \times 100 = 600$

$6 \times 3000 = 6 \times 3 \times 1000 = 18 \times 1000 = 18000$

$18 \times 4000 = 18 \times 4 \times 1000 = 72 \times 1000 = 72000$

Exercise 5.2

1. Complete the following

a. $70 \times 100 =$ ______

b. $19 \times 3000 =$ ______

c. $24 \times 800 =$ ______

d. $30 \times 3000 =$ ______

e. $10 \times 5000 =$ ______

f. $4 \times 4000 =$ ______

g. $110 \times 6000 =$ ______

h. $138 \times 200 =$ ______

i. $16 \times 600 =$ ______

j. $120 \times 1000 =$ ______

2. Find the product

a. 305×4000

b. 137×2000

c. 16×600

d. 39×900

e. 25×3000

f. 26×200

g. 214×3000

h. 365×700

i. 40×200

j. 72×300

Multiplication by a 2-digit number

EXAMPLE

	H	T	O	
	4	6	8	← Multiplicand
	×	2	7	← Multiplier
3	2	7	6	
9	3	6	0	
1 2	6	3	6	

27 = 20+7

468x7 = 3276

468x20 = 9360

12636

Multiplication by a 3-digit number

EXAMPLE

Multiplication by a 3-digit number is the same as multiplying by a 2-digit number.

			H	T	O	
			2	8	7	← Multiplicand
		×	3	4	5	← Multiplier 300 + 40 + 5
		1	4	3	5	← 287 x 5
	1	1	4	8	0	← 287 x 40
	8	6	1	0	0	← 287 x 300
	9	9	0	1	5	

287 is the multiplicand, 345 the multiplier and 99015 the product

Exercise 5.3

1. Fill in the boxes and find the product.

648	
× 257	
4536	648 × ☐
32400	648 × ☐
129600	648 × ☐
	648 × ☐

139	
× 246	
834	☐ × 6
5560	☐ × 40
27800	139 × ☐
	139 × ☐

2. Find the product

a. 277 x163	b. 425 x138	c. 698 x245	d. 786 x291	e. 473 x580
f. 991 x106	g. 309 x724	h. 620 x158	i. 592 x208	j. 803 x210
k. 635 x350	l. 869 x473	m. 254 x124	n. 679 x412	o. 525 x120

Word Problems

175 people can sit in one compartment of a train. How many people can sit in 18 such compartments?

Number of people in 1 compartment = 175

Number of compartments = 18

Total number of people = 175 × 18

= 3150

H	T	O
1	7	5

```
   1 7 5
   x 1 8
 1 4 0 0
 1 7 5 0
 3 1 5 0
```

Exercise 5.4

1. Solve the following word problems.
   a. The cost of a mobile is ₹ 8750. Find the cost of 204 such mobiles.
   b. A factory produces 3842 bicycles in a day. How many bicycles are produced in the month of March?
   c. A group of 295 children went to visit a theme park. Each child had to pay ₹ 320 as entry fees. What was the total amount spent as fees?
   d. Tata Motors manufactures 2574 cars every month. How many cars would be manufactured in 2 years 4 months?
   e. A bank collected 1230 five hundred rupee notes on a particular day. How much money was collected on that day?
   f. A truck can carry 130 bags of cement. How many bags of cement will 264 such trucks carry?
   g. Find the product of the largest 4-digit number and the largest 3-digit number.
   h. How many hours are there in the month of August?

Estimating Products

When an exact answer is not required, we can estimate the product by rounding off numbers.

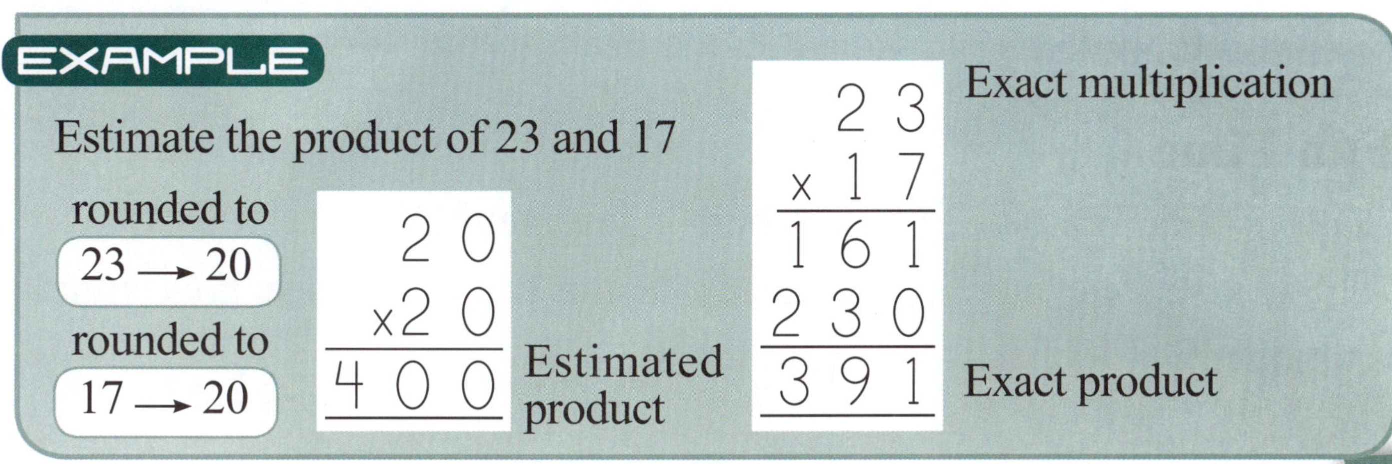

EXAMPLE

Estimate the product of 23 and 17

425 → 400	400 x 100
137 → 100	= 40,000
	Estimated product

$$\begin{array}{r} 425 \\ \times 137 \\ \hline 2975 \\ 12750 \\ 42500 \\ \hline 58225 \end{array}$$ Exact product

Exercise 5.5

Estimate as indicated

1. Round off to the nearest 10

a.	25 × 28	e.	95 × 8
b.	42 × 56	f.	71 × 57
c.	32 × 64	g.	27 × 83
d.	38 × 12	h.	88 × 28

2. Rounding off to the nearest 100

a.	364 × 275	e.	742 × 384
b.	636 × 248	f.	309 × 121
c.	655 × 706	g.	451 × 142
d.	216 × 605	h.	426 × 265

Fun Time

Maths is fun. The beauty of numbers is fascinating.

'11' is a strange number. When 11 is the multiplier see how simple multiplication with a 2-digit number is.

EXAMPLE

$$\begin{array}{r} 43 \\ \times 11 \\ \hline 473 \\ \hline \end{array}$$

Step1: Write 4 in hundreds place
Step2: Write 3 in ones place
Step3: (4+3) in tens place
So, 43 × 11 = 473

EXAMPLE

$$\begin{array}{r} 36 \\ \times 11 \\ \hline 396 \\ \hline \end{array}$$

Step1: Write 3 in hundreds place
Step2: Write 6 in ones place
Step3: (3+6) in tens place
So, 36 × 11 = 396

EXAMPLE

$$\begin{array}{r} 75 \\ \times 11 \\ \hline 825 \\ \hline \end{array}$$

Step1: Write 7 in hundreds place
Step2: Write 5 in ones place
Step3: (7+5) in tens place
So, 75 × 11 = 825 (Add 1 to hundreds place)

EXAMPLE

$$\begin{array}{r} 86 \\ \times 11 \\ \hline 946 \\ \hline \end{array}$$

Step1: Write 8 in hundreds place
Step2: Write 6 in ones place
Step3: (8+6) in tens place
So, 86 × 11 = 946 (Add 1 to hundreds place)
Product is 946

Now you can try with a few numbers on your own 58×11, 49×11 etc.

Mental Maths

1. Fill in the missing numbers.

   a. 70 × ________ = 1400000

   b. ________ × 800 = 72000000

   c. 98 × 6000 = 98 × ________ × 1000

   d. 209 × 7000 = 209 × 7 × ________

   e. 297 × 5000 = 297 × 5 × ________

   f. ________ × 300 = 10500

2. What will be product if we multiply double of 263 by the triple of 3000?

3. What will be the product if we multiply by the double of 500 by the difference between 3518 and 2675?

4. If 200 × A = 18000 then A is ________

5. B × B = 490000, then B = ________

Division

6

Division is repeated subtraction or equal distribution of a given quantity.

EXAMPLE

$$
\begin{array}{rl}
32 & \\
-\ 4 & \\
\hline
28 & 1^{st} \\
-\ 4 & \\
\hline
24 & 2^{nd} \\
-\ 4 & \\
\hline
20 & 3^{rd} \\
-\ 4 & \\
\hline
16 & 4^{th}
\end{array}
\qquad
\begin{array}{rl}
16 & \\
-\ 4 & \\
\hline
12 & 5^{th} \\
-\ 4 & \\
\hline
8 & 6^{th} \\
-\ 4 & \\
\hline
4 & 7^{th} \\
-\ 4 & \\
\hline
0 & 8^{th} \\
\hline
\end{array}
$$

Long division

$$
\begin{array}{r|l}
 & 8 \rightarrow \text{Quotient} \\
4 & 32 \ \ \text{Dividend} \\
 & -32 \ \ \text{Divisor} \\
 & \text{x} \ \ \text{Remainder}
\end{array}
$$

Hence, she had 8 friends

Division Facts

$8 \times 4 = 32$

So $32 \div 4 = 8$

Some facts about division

If a number is divided by 1, the quotient is the number itself.

1. $14 \div 1 = 14$
2. $28 \div 28 = 1$

A number when divided by itself gives quotient 1.

3. $0 \div 264 = 0$

$0 \div 4 = 0$

If zero is divided by any number the quotient is always 0.

4. $6 \times 8 = 48$; $48 \div 6 = 8$ and $48 \div 8 = 6$

In division, the remainder should always be smaller than the divisor.

Every multiplication fact has two division facts.

Exercise 6.1

1. Fill in the blanks

a. $0 \div 24 =$ ________

b. ________ $\div 15 = 0$

c. $234 \div$ ________ $= 1$

d. $3269 \div 3269 =$ ________

e. If $9 \times 5 = 45$; so ________ $\div 5 =$ ________ and $45 \div 9 =$ ________

f. If $56 \div 8 = 7$ the other division fact is ________

g. $70 \div 7 =$ ________

h. $21 \div 3 =$ ________

i. $63 \div 7 =$ ________

j. $81 \div 9 =$ ________

k. $56 \div 8 =$ ________

l. $54 \div 6 =$ ________

m. $72 \div 9 =$ ________

n. $80 \div 10 =$ ________

o. $36 \div 4 =$ ________

Multiplication by 100 and division by 100

16	×	100	=	1600	1600	÷	100	=	16
284	×	100	=	28400	28400	÷	100	=	284
30	×	100	=	3000	3000	÷	100	=	30

Hence, When we divide a number which ends in 2 zeroes by 100, we remove the 2 zeroes and get the quotient.

Observe this

8 × 4	=	32	32 ÷ 8	=	4
8 × 40	=	320	320 ÷ 8	=	40
8 × 400	=	3200	3200 ÷ 8	=	400
8 × 4000	=	32000	32000 ÷ 8	=	4000

Now, fill in the blanks

63	÷ 9	=	7	72	÷ 12	=	6
630	÷ 9	=	70	720	÷ 12	=	
6300	÷ 9	=		7200	÷ 12	=	
63000	÷ 9	=		72000	÷ 12	=	6000
630000	÷ 9	=		720000	÷ 12	=	

Exercise 6.2

1. Find the quotient mentally without actually dividing.

a. $60 \div 10$	e. $7300 \div 100$	i. $360 \div 10$
b. $4800 \div 10$	f. $76300 \div 100$	j. $5200 \div 10$
c. $2780 \div 10$	g. $3000 \div 100$	k. $1400 \div 100$
d. $800 \div 100$	h. $9040 \div 10$	l. $5100 \div 100$

Division by long method (Long division method)

EXAMPLE

Divide 342 by 6

```
     H T O
       5 7
    ________
 6 ) 3 4 2
    -3 0
    ______
       4 2
      -4 2
    ______
       x x
    ______
```

Step 1: $3 < 6$, so, take 34 tens as the dividend

$6 \times 5 = 30 < 34$

$6 \times 6 = 36 > 34$

Step 2: So, take $6 \times 5 = 30$ and

Write 30 below 34.

Step 3: Save $34 - 30 = 4$

Bring down 2.

$7 \times 6 = 42$

Division with remainder

EXAMPLE

Divide 408 by 7

```
     H T O
       5 8
    ________
 7 ) 4 0 8
    -3 5
    ______
     x 5 8
      -5 6
    ______
         2 ← Remainder
    ______
```

Exercise 6.3

1. Divide by long division method, mention the quotient and remainder.

a. $76 \div 3$	e. $98 \div 2$	i. $68 \div 5$	m. $432 \div 3$
b. $143 \div 7$	f. $707 \div 9$	j. $440 \div 8$	n. $339 \div 6$
c. $704 \div 5$	g. $5832 \div 7$	k. $3293 \div 4$	o. $4712 \div 9$
d. $6030 \div 8$	h. $9802 \div 6$	l. $982 \div 7$	p. $8623 \div 8$

Division by 10, 100, 1000

Let us check a few products and their division facts

$4 \times 10 = 40$	$60 \times 10 = 600$	$15 \times 10 = 150$
$40 \div 10 = 4$	$600 \div 10 = 60$	$150 \div 10 = 15$

So, when we divide a number ending in a zero by 10, we have to remove the zero in the ones place to get the quotient.

Divison by 2-digit number

Divison by a 2-digit number is the same as division by a single digit number.

EXAMPLE

Divide 2458 by 18

Step 1: $2 < 18$ take 24

$18 \times 1 = 18$

Write 1 in Hundreds place in the quotient.

Write 18 below 24 and subtract

$24 - 18 = 6$

Step 2: Bring down 5

$18 \times 3 = 54$

And $18 \times 4 = 72 > 65$

```
       H T O
       1 3 6
   ---------
18 ) 2 4 5 8
    -1 8
    ----
       6 5
      -5 4
      ----
       1 1 8
      -1 0 8
      ------
Remainder → 1 0
```

We have to write a product less than 65. So we write 3 in tens place in the quotient. Write 54 below 65 & then subtract.

Step 3: $18 \times 6 = 108$

$18 \times 7 = 126$

$126 > 118$

Write 108 below 118, sub Remainder = 10

Dividend = Divisor × Quotient + Remainder

EXAMPLE

Divide 4679 by 31

Step1: $2 < 31$ Take 26. $26 < 31$ so, take 267

$31 \times 8 = 248$

$31 \times 9 = 279$

$248 < 267$

Write 248 below 267 and 8 in tens place (for quotient)

Step2: Bring down 9

$31 \times 6 = 186$

Write 6 in ones place in Quotient

Write 186 below 199 & subtract

```
      H T O
        8 6
    ---------
31 )  2679
     -248 ↓
     -----
       199
      -186
      ----
        13
      ----
```

Q = 86

R = 13

Exercise 6.4

1. Solve the following to find the quotient and the remainder:

a. $75 \div 13$	e. $98 \div 42$	i. $331 \div 13$	m. $315 \div 28$
b. $680 \div 34$	f. $709 \div 36$	j. $205 \div 23$	n. $652 \div 47$
c. $7192 \div 27$	g. $2932 \div 17$	k. $7225 \div 25$	o. $3037 \div 39$
d. $5763 \div 61$	h. $444 \div 22$	l. $7070 \div 11$	p. $4396 \div 35$

2. 1893 ÷ 49 gives 38 quotient and 31 as remainder. Using this fill in blanks without dividing or multiplying.

   a. 49 × 38 = ________

   b. 38 × ________ + 31 = 1893

   c. 1895 ÷ 49 gives quotient 38 and remainder ________

   d. 1888 ÷ 49 gives quotient 38 and remainder ________

Division by 10, 100, 1000

Division	Quotient	Remainder
74 ÷ 10	7	4
525 ÷ 100	5	25
608 ÷ 100	6	8
4984 ÷ 100	49	84
6380 ÷ 1000	6	380
5021 ÷ 1000	5	21
2165 ÷ 100	21	65

Look at the pattern. When a number is divided by 100, the remainder is the number formed by digits in the tens and ones place.

The quotient is the number formed by remaining last two digits.

When a number is divided by 1000, the quotient is the number without the last three digits, the remainder is the number formed by the digits in hundreds, tens and ones place.

Exercise 6.5

1. Find the quotient and remainder

a. 5460 ÷ 100	e. 4070 ÷ 1000	i. 25600 ÷ 1000
b. 686 ÷ 10	f. 7000 ÷ 1000	j. 4280 ÷ 1000
c. 12634 ÷ 1000	g. 9000 ÷ 100	k. 3040 ÷ 1000
d. 3905 ÷ 10	h. 9086 ÷ 100	l. 6875 ÷ 1000

Word Problems

There are 4680 refreshment packets which are to be distributed in 18 schools equally. How many packets will each school get?

Total packets to be distributed = 4680

No. of schools = 18

No. of packets distributed in each school = 4680 ÷ 18

= 260

```
        HTO
        260
18 ) 4680
    -36
     108
    -108
     xxx0
        0
        x
```

EXAMPLE

Product of two numbers is 15138. If one of them is 29 find the other number.

Solution

Product of two numbers is = 15138

One number is = 29

Second number is 15138 ÷ 29

= 522

```
          HTO
          522
29 ) 15138
    -145
     0063
      -58
      058
      -58
       xx
```

Exercise 6.6

Solve the following word problems

1. 915 books had to he packed in boxes. If 25 books were to be packed in a box, how many boxes would be needed to pack all the books?
2. Raja took 194 sweets to school. He distributed it to 36 students of his class? How many did each child get? How many were left with Raja?
3. A shopkeeper bought 835 eggs. 43 were broken. He packed the remaining in 33 boxes. How many eggs were there in each box?
4. 4630 pamphlets were distributed in 34 colonies. If each colony got same number, how many pamphlets were given in each colony. Were there any left over?
5. 575 chairs were distributed equally in 23 class rooms. How many chairs did each class get?
6. The product of two numbers is 3052. If one number is 28, find the other number?
7. Sunita reads 35 pages every day. How many days will she take to read a book of 864 pages? How many pages will she read on the last day?
8. 25 watches cost ₹ 17000. Find the cost of 1 watch.
9. In an orchard there were 7623 mango trees in 11 rows. What is the number of trees in each row, if the number in every row was the same?

Estimating the quotient

Estimate the quotient

1. 94 ÷ 26

   This is rounded off

   as 90 ÷ 30 = 3

2. 536 ÷ 26

   This is rounded off as

   540 ÷ 30 = 18

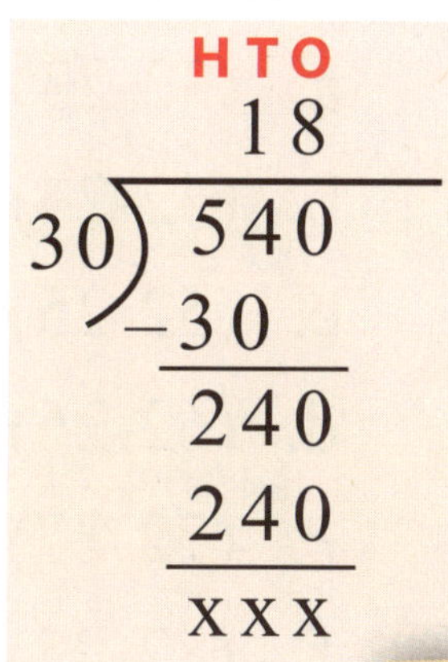

Exercise 6.7

1. Find the estimated quotient

a. 83 ÷ 23 b. 57 ÷ 18 c. 192 ÷ 24

d. 520 ÷ 28 e. 704 ÷ 21

Patterns in division

1. Maths is wonderful! Observe the pattern and fill in the blanks. Remember, if the dividend increases, so does the quotient (keeping divisor the same)

a. 8 ÷ 4 = 2

b. 80 ÷ 4 = 20

c. 800 ÷ 4 = 200

d. 80, 00 ÷ 4 = ________

e. 80, 000 ÷ 4 = ________

f. 8, 00, 00 ÷ 4 = ________

2. If the divisor increases, quotient decreases (keeping dividend the same)

a. 20, 000 ÷ 5 = 4, 000

b. 20,000 ÷ 50 = 400

c. 20,000 ÷ 500 = ________

d. 20,000 ÷ 5000 = ________

3. If one tens and one ones is increased each time (keeping divisor the same)

a. (32-23) ÷ 9 = 1

b. (42-24) ÷ 9 = 2

c. (52-25) ÷ 9 = 3

d. (62-26) ÷ 9 = ______

e. (72-27) ÷ 9 = ______

f. (82-28) ÷ 9 = ______

4. Observe the pattern.

a. $11 \div 11 = 1$

b. $121 \div 11 = 11$

c. $12321 \div 111 = 111$

d. $1234321 \div 1111 = 1111$

e. $123454321 \div 11111 = 11111$

5. Observe the pattern.

a. $1 \times 9 + 2 = 11$

b. $12 \times 9 + 3 = 111$

c. $123 \times 9 + 4 = 1111$

d. ____ $\times 9 + 5 = 11111$

e. ____ $\times 9 +$ ____ $= 111111$

Mental Maths

1. $78345 \div$ ______ $= 1$

2. ______ $\div 1 = 26943$

3. $180460 \div 18046 =$ ______

4. ______ $\div 4507 = 100$

5. Find the quotient if one tenth of the smallest 6-digit number is divided by one-fifth of the smallest 3-digit number.

6. $235235 \div 235 = 100 +$ ______

7. In a herd, for 8 cows there is a buffalo. If there are 54 animals in the herd, then number of cows is ______ and number of buffaloes is ______ .

Multiples and Factors

7

Multiples

Fill in the blanks to complete the multiplication facts tables.

1×1	=		1×3	=		1×8	=	
2×1	=		2×3	=		2×8	=	
3×1	=		3×3	=		3×8	=	
4×1	=		4×3	=		4×8	=	
5×1	=		5×3	=		5×8	=	
6×1	=		6×3	=		6×8	=	
7×1	=		7×3	=		7×8	=	

These are the tables of 1, 3 and 8 (Up to 7th place) and the numbers in the boxes are called the **multiples**.

So, if we write $3 \times 5 = 15$

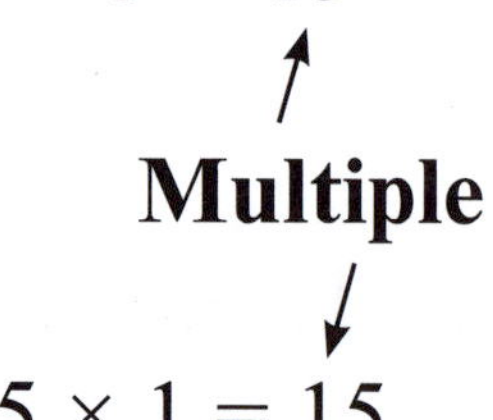

$15 \times 1 = 15$

If $4 \times 6 = 24$, then 24 is the multiple. Look at the grid in the next page.

×	1	2	3	4	5	6	7	8	9	10	11	12
2	2	4	6	8	10	12	14	16	18	20	22	24
3	3	6	9	12	15	18	21	24	27	30	33	36
4	4	8	12	16	20	24	28	32	36	40	44	48
5	5	10	15	20	25	30	35	40	45	50	55	60
6	6	12	18	24	30	36	42	48	54	60	66	72
7	7	14	21	28	35	42	49	56	63	70	77	84
8	8	16	24	32	40	48	56	64	72	80	88	96
9	9	18	27	36	45	54	63	72	81	90	99	108
10	10	20	30	40	50	60	70	80	90	100	110	120

1. We can see multiples 2, 3, 4, 5, 6, 7, 8, 9, 10, 11, 12 in this grid are written in black. Many numbers appear more than once. Answer the following questions by looking at the grid —

   a. 6 is a multiple of 2. 6 is also a multiple of ____ and ____.

   b. 20 is a multiple of ____, ____, ____, ____, and ____.

   c. Multiples of 7 less than 30 are ____, ____, ____, and ____.

   d. ____ is a multiple of 7 and 8.

   e. ____ and ____ are multiples of 2 , 3 and 4.

   f. Every number is a multiple of ____ and ____.

Facts about multiples

$4 \times 5 = 20$

20 is a multiple of 4 and 5.

$2 \times 1 = 2$ $\quad$ $5 \times 1 = 5$

2 is a multiple of 2 and 1

5 is a multiple of 5 and 1

Hence, every number is a multiple of 1.

Every number in a multiple of itself.

$4 \times 3 = \mathbf{12}$ $\quad$ $5 \times 6 = \mathbf{30}$ $\quad$ $10 \times 1 = \mathbf{10}$

Here, we see 12 is a multiple of 4 and 3 and $12 > 4$, $12 > 3$

30 is a multiple of 5 and 6 and $30 > 5$, $30 > 6$

10 is a multiple of 1 and 10 and $10 > 1$, $10 = 10$

Every multiple is greater than or equal to the number.

Multiples can go on, there is no end to it.

Odd and even number

A number which is a multiple of 2 is called an **even number**

2, 4, 6, 8, 10, 12, ... are even numbers.

A number which is not a multiple of 2 is an **odd number**

Example 1, 3, 5, 7, 9, 11, ... are odd numbers.

Even numbers have 0, 2, 4, 6, 8 in ones place.
Odd numbers have 1, 3, 5, 7, 9 in ones place.

Exercise 7.1

1. Fill in the multiples of:

   a. 10 → 10, 20, ________, ________, ________, ________

   b. 4 → 4, 8, ________, ________, ________, ________

   c. 8 → 8, ________, ________, ________, ________

   d. 11 → 11, ________, ________, ________, ________

   e. 7 → 7, ________, ________, ________, ________

2. Fill in the blanks in the sentences given below.

   a. $3 \times 7 = 21$ 21 is a multiple of ______ and 7.

   b. $4 \times$ __ $= 36$ 36 is a multiple of ______ and ______.

   c. __ $\times 8 = 72$ ___ is a multiple of 8 and ______.

   d. $7 \times$ ___ $= 49$ ___ is a multiple of _____.

   e. $1 \times$ ___ $= 1$ 1 is the multiple of _____.

3. Circle the even numbers.

   6, 13, 11, 14, 7, 19, 21, 1

4. Circle the odd numbers.

   16, 9, 5, 15, 60, 61, 55, 50

5. Check if the first number is the multiple of

the 2nd number, give your answer in Yes / No.

   a. 36, 9 b. 42, 8 c. 88, 9

   d. 15, 5 e. 72, 8

Factors

Multiple of 4 and 5 ⟶ $4 \times 5 = 20$

20 is a multiple of 4 and 5.

4 and 5 are called factors of 20.

$\underline{7 \times 6} = \underline{42}$

Factors of 42 (pointing to 7 × 6); Multiple of 7 and 6 (pointing to 42)

Find factors of 16

$1 \times 16 = 16$, 1 and 16 are factors of 16

$2 \times 8 = 16$, 2 and 8 are factors of 16

$4 \times 4 = 16$, 4 is a factor of 16

So, factors of 16 are 1, 2, 4, 8, 16

Let us explore factors of some more numbers.

EXAMPLE

Find factors of

a. 1 b. 7 c. 21

a. $1 \times 1 = 1$ 1 has only one factor, 1 itself

b. $1 \times 7 = 7$ 7 has only 2 factors 1 and 7

c. $1 \times 21 = 21$ 21 has factors 1, 3, 7 and 21

$3 \times 7 = 21$

When we multiply 2 or more numbers, we get a product. This product is the multiple of each of the numbers multiplied.

Each number (that is multiplied) is a factor of the multiple (product).

Finding factors

Let us take some number say 12 and see its factors.

Factor Product

$1 \times 12 = 12$ $5 \times ? = 12 \longrightarrow$ 5 is not a factor of 12.

$2 \times 6 = 12$

$3 \times 4 = 12$

So, factors of 12 are 1, 2, 3, 4, 6 and 12

We see that the smallest factor is 1 and greatest is 12, the number itself.

Is there any other method to find factors? Since factors are divisible by a given number, let us explore if we can find factors by division.

EXAMPLE

Find factors of 24 by division.

Number DIVISOR		Quotient
$24 \div 1$	=	24
$24 \div 2$	=	12
$24 \div 3$	=	8
$24 \div 4$	=	6
$24 \div 5$	$\longrightarrow$	cannot divide exactly
$24 \div 6$	=	4

All divisors and quotients are factors, when factors are repeated no further division is carried out.

Factors of 24 are 1, 2, 3, 4, 6, 8, 12 and 24.

Facts about factors

1. 1 is a factor of every number.
2. The greatest factor of a number is the number itself
3. Some numbers have only 2 factors. Some have more than 2 factors.

Exercise 7.2

1. List all the factors of the following numbers

a. 25	d. 36	g. 18	i. 11
b. 20	e. 45	h. 50	j. 5
c. 23	f. 17		

2. Is the second number a factor of the first? (show it)

   a. 45, 7

   b. 120, 6

   c. 150, 8

   d. 214, 10

3. Fill in the blanks

   a. ________, _________ and _________ are factors of 10.

   b. ___________ is a factor of every number.

   c. The greatest factor of a number is the __________.

   d. When a number is divided by its factor, the remainder is __________.

   e. 5 is a factor of _________ (choose from 1, 5, 14, 20, 27, 30, 35)

   f. The number of factors of a number are __________ (limited/ unlimited)

4. Shade the factors of the central numbers.

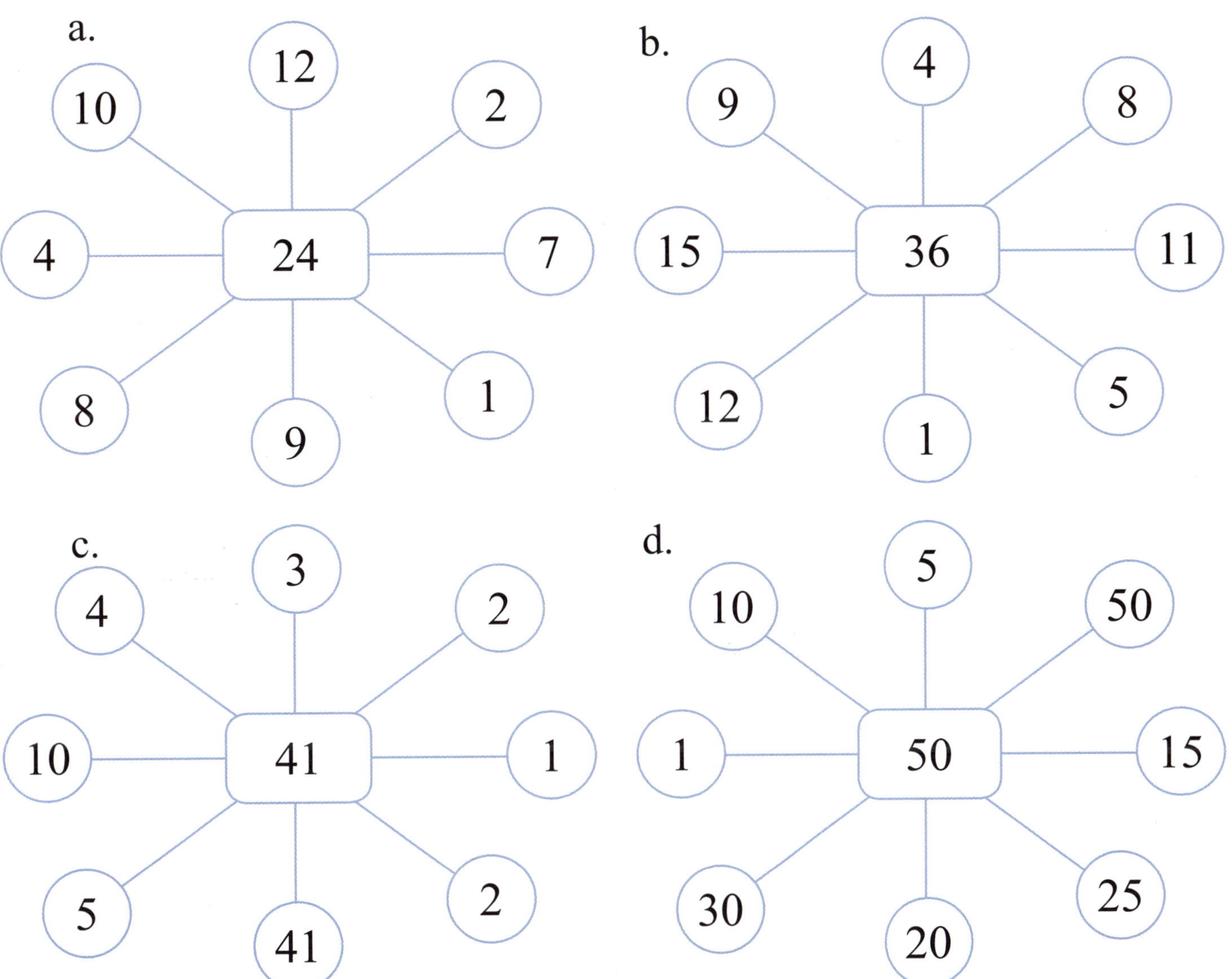

Real Life Situation

A child has 36 books. He wants to stack them in piles of equal size. How many such piles are possible? How will he do it?

Solution

Knowledge of factors and multiples will help him. He will check

$1 \times 36 = 36$ can have 1 pile of 36 books or 36 books piled up separately

$2 \times 18 = 36$ 2 piles of18 books each or 18 piles of 2 books each

$9 \times 4 = 36$ 4 piles of 9 books each or 9 piles of 4 books each

$6 \times 6 = 36$ 6 piles of 6 books each

Prime and Composite Numbers

Number	Factors	Number	Factors
1	1	(11)	1, 11
(2)	1, 2	12	1, 2, 4, 6, 12
(3)	1, 3	(13)	1, 13
4	1, 2, 4	14	
(5)	1, 5	15	
6	1, 2, 3, 6	16	
(7)	1, 7	(17)	
8	1, 2, 4, 8	18	
9	1, 3, 9	(19)	
10	1, 2, 5, 10	20	

We see there are some numbers which have only 2 factors and the others have more than 2 factors.

In a number which has 2 factors, we see that it is 1 and the number itself.

Such numbers which have only 2 factors are called Prime Numbers.

2, 3, 5, 7, 11, 13, 17, 19... (The circled numbers of the table)

The numbers which have more than 2 factors are called Composite Numbers.

Exercise 7.3

1. Fill in the blanks

   a. ________ is a factor of every number.

   b. Every prime number has ________factors.

   c. ________ has only 1 factor

   d. ________ number has more than 2 factors.

   e. ________ is neither prime nor composite.

   f. 59 is a prime number. Its factors are ________.

2. List all prime numbers between

   a. 1 and 15   b. 20 and 40

3. Find composite numbers between

   a. 1 to 20   b. 30 to 50

4. 13 and 31 are both primes and are formed by the same digits.
   Find more pairs of 2-digit prime numbers having the same digits.

Common factors

Factors of 12 are (1) 2 (3) 4 5 6 12

Factors of 15 are (1) 3 (5) 15

Common factors are 1 and 3

Exercise 7.4

Numbers	Factors	Common
10	1, 2, 5, 10	1, 2, 5
15	1, 2, 3, 5, 15	
24		
32		
18		
35		
42		
60		

Divisible numbers

$32 \div 8 = 4$ $\qquad$ $32 \div 5 = $ Q 6, R = 2

$48 \div 6 = 8$ $\qquad$ $48 \div 9 = $ Q 5, R = 3

We say 32 is divisible by 8 but 32 is not divisible by 5.

48 is divisible by 6 but it is not divisible by 9

A number is divisible by another number if on dividing it, the remainder is 0.

Tests of Divisibility

Tests of divisibility is a quick way to check whether a number is divisible by another number (without actually dividing)

Divisibility by 2

For a number to be divisible by 2, the digit in the ones place should be 0, 2, 4, 6, 8 [The number should be even]

EXAMPLE

68 → is divisible by 2

369 → not divisible by 2

Divisibility by 5

All numbers ending in 0 or 5 are divisible by 5.

EXAMPLE

53 → not divisible by 5

365 → divisible by 5

2170 → divisible by 5

Divisibility by 10

All numbers ending with 0 are divisible by 10.

Example 60, 370, 4070 etc

Divisibility by 3

Some numbers divisible by 3 are 15, 18, 27

15 $1 + 5 = 6$ → multiple of 3

18 $1 + 8 = 9$ → multiple of 3

27 $2 + 7 = 9$ → multiple of 3

A number is divisible by 3, if the sum of the digits of that number is a multiple of 3.

EXAMPLE

3207 → $3 + 2 + 0 + 7 = 13$ is not a multiple of 3.

Hence, 3207 is not divisible by 3

5346 → $5 + 3 + 4 + 6 = 18$ is multiple of 3

So, 5346 is divisible by 3

Divisibility by 6

12 is divisible by 2 and 3

12 is also divisible by 6

36 is also divisible by 2 and 3

therefore ⟶ 36 is divisible by 6

A number is divisible by 6 if it is divisible by 2 and 3 both.

EXAMPLE

348 ⟶ is an even number

$3 + 4 + 8 = 15$ ⟶ multiple of 3

348 is divisible by 6 as it is divisible by 2 and 3 both.

Exercise 7.5

1. Circle the numbers divisible by 2

   1 2 4 9 57 88 123 324

2. Circle the numbers divisible by 3

   5 10 55 53 96 80 103

3. Tick (✓) the numbers divisible by 3

   a. 23 ☐

   b. 52 ☐

   c. 45 ☐

4. Which of the following numbers are multiple of 6?

   36 102 75 72 92 98 900 3060

5. Complete the table

Number	Divisible by				
	2	3	5	6	10
518	✓	×	×	×	×
4320					
1000					
600					
90					
80					
10					

6. Do as directed

a. Write the multiples of 5 from 19 to 38

b. Write the prime numbers from 21 to 30

c. Write the number divisible by 5 and 10 both, from 15 to 66.

7. Complete the following.

a. 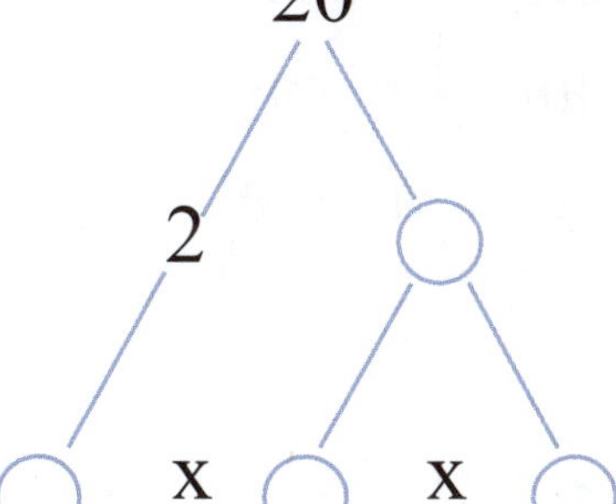

b. 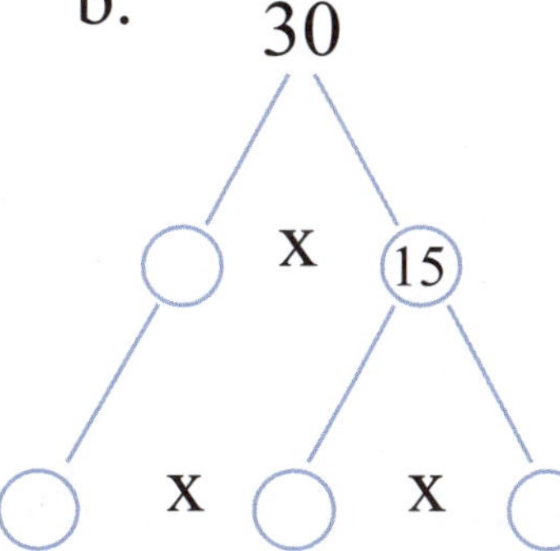

Activity

Factors and Multiples

Materials required: Square counters; paper

[if not available squares should be given]

Divide the class into groups of 4

Each group should have about 25-30 counters.

Teacher should ask them to arrange a particular number like 12 or 16 or 20 in different ways.

1 row of 16 counters

$1 \times 16 = 16$

2 rows of 8 each

$2 \times 8 = 16$

4 rows of 4 each

Teacher should relate this to problems as well

Students should arrange for other numbers like 18, 20, 24 etc.

When the counters are arranged, students would be able to relate to the concept of area (of rectangles and squares)

Fractions

If a pizza is cut into two equal parts each is ½ or half of the whole pizza.

$\frac{1}{2}$ $\frac{1}{2}$

A bar of chocolate into 4 equal parts

$\frac{1}{4}$ = one fourth

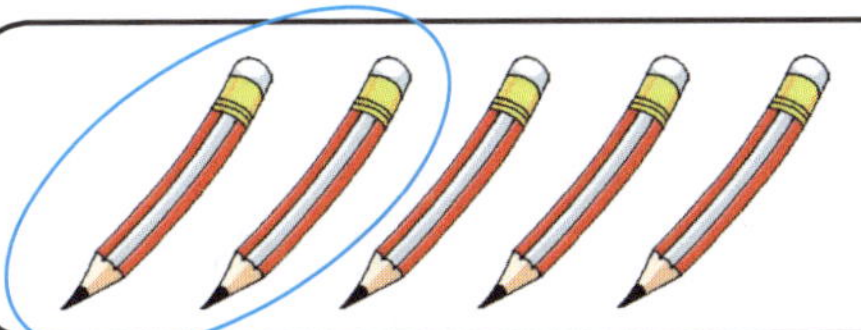

2 out of 5 is 2/5 or two fifth of pencils

A fraction is an equal part or parts of a whole or a group.

Exercise 8.1

1. Write the fraction for the shaded part.

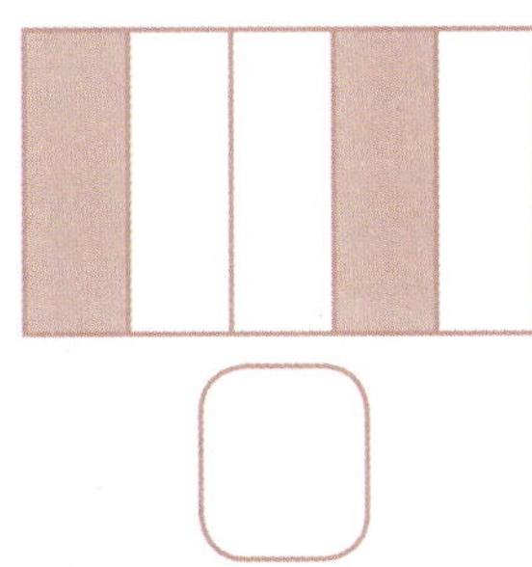

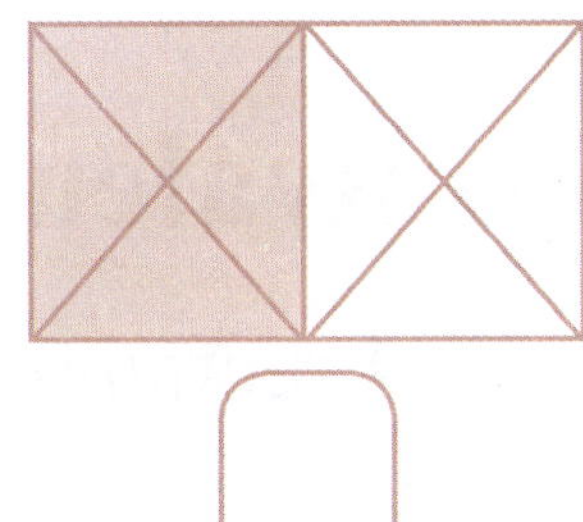

2. Shade the part of each whole as indicated in the box below:

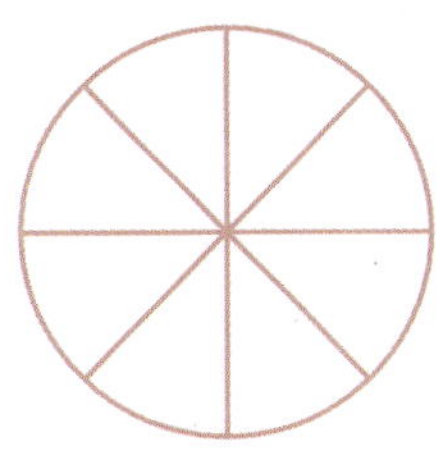

$\frac{5}{8}$

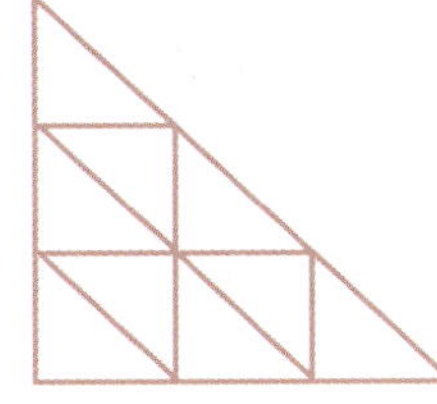

$\frac{3}{9}$

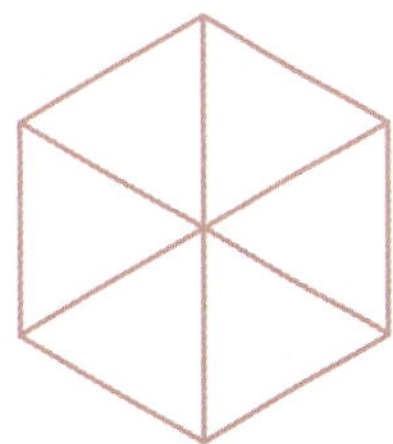

$\frac{6}{6}$

$\frac{2}{7}$

3. Write the fraction for the part mentioned.

   a. A cake was cut into 12 equal pieces. Each child ate 2 pieces. What fraction of cake did each child get? ☐

   b. A group of students was divided into 4 equal groups. All the girls were in 1 group. What fraction of the group were girls. ☐

4. Fill in the blanks

	Fraction	Numerator	Denominator	Name
a.	$\frac{3}{7}$	3		Three seventh
b.	$\frac{4}{11}$			
c.	$\frac{7}{13}$			Seven–thirteenth
d.	$\frac{6}{23}$			
e.	$\frac{8}{100}$			

Equivalent Fractions

Take 4 rectangular pieces of paper of the same size.

1. Divide the first into 2 equal parts shade $\frac{1}{2}$

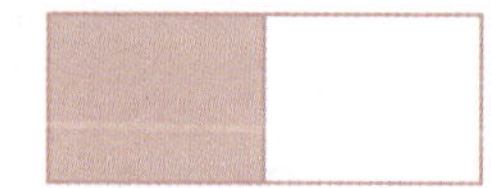

2. Divide the second into 4 equal parts as shown. Shade $\frac{2}{4}$

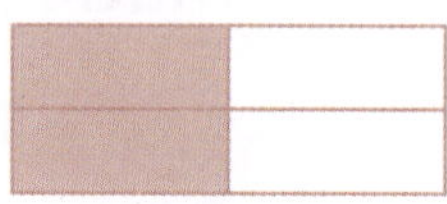

3. Divide the 3rd into 8 equal parts. Shade $\frac{4}{8}$ parts

4. Divide the fourth piece into 16 equal parts and shade $\frac{8}{16}$ parts.

In all the four cases, the shaded portion is the same (half of the piece)

$\frac{1}{2}$ is the same as $\frac{2}{4}$ $\frac{4}{8}$ $\frac{8}{16}$

The value of the fraction in all the four cases is the same.

The fractions which have equal value are called **equivalent fractions**.

Building Equivalent Fractions

1. Multiplying the numerator and the denominat by the same number

$$\frac{2}{3} = \frac{2 \times 2}{3 \times 2} = \frac{4}{6}$$

$$\frac{2}{3} = \frac{2 \times 3}{3 \times 3} = \frac{6}{9}$$

$$\frac{2}{3} = \frac{2 \times 5}{3 \times 5} = \frac{10}{15}$$

so, $\frac{2}{3}$, $\frac{4}{6}$, $\frac{6}{9}$, $\frac{10}{15}$ are equivalent fractions.

2. Dividing the numerator and denominator by the same number.

$$\frac{16}{32} = \frac{16 \div 2}{32 \div 2} = \frac{8}{16}$$

$$\frac{16}{32} = \frac{16 \div 4}{32 \div 4} = \frac{4}{8}$$

$$\frac{16}{32} = \frac{16 \div 16}{32 \div 16} = \frac{1}{2}$$

$\frac{16}{32}$, $\frac{8}{16}$, $\frac{4}{8}$, $\frac{1}{2}$ are equivalent fractions.

Exercise 8.2

1. Look at the figures and fill in the boxes.

a.

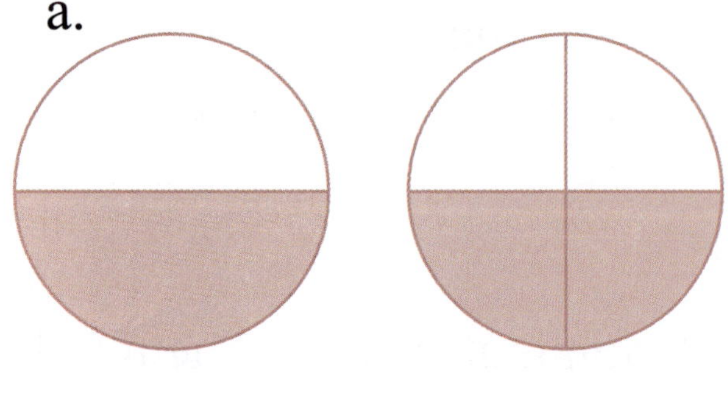

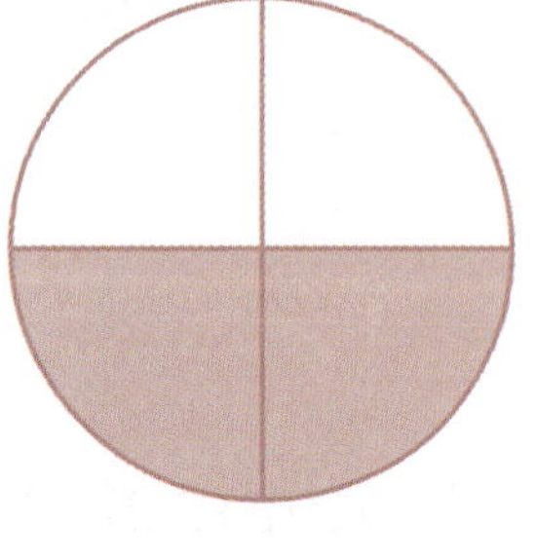

$\frac{1}{2}$ $\frac{\square}{4}$

b.

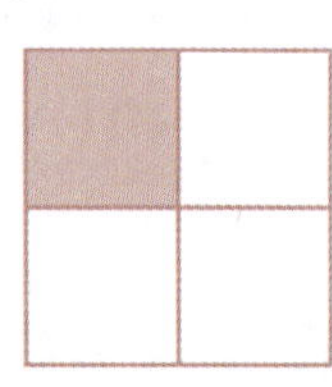

$\frac{1}{4}$ $\frac{\square}{\square}$

2. Circle the equivalent fractions.

a. $\frac{2}{3} \longrightarrow \frac{4}{6} \quad \frac{5}{15} \quad \frac{8}{12} \quad \frac{10}{12}$

b. $\frac{1}{6} \longrightarrow \frac{2}{12} \quad \frac{3}{18} \quad \frac{4}{40} \quad \frac{5}{30}$

c. $\frac{3}{4} \longrightarrow \frac{30}{40} \quad \frac{9}{12} \quad \frac{6}{2} \quad \frac{9}{2}$

3. Fill in the boxes in these equivalent fractions.

a. $\frac{1}{2} = \frac{\square}{6}$

i. $\frac{4}{6} = \frac{\square}{3}$

b. $\frac{\square}{3} = \frac{6}{9}$

j. $\frac{\square}{1} = \frac{8}{8}$

c. $\frac{\square}{7} = \frac{2}{14}$

d. $\frac{1}{4} = \frac{5}{\square}$

e. $\frac{4}{5} = \frac{40}{\square}$

f. $\frac{\square}{14} = \frac{36}{56}$

g. $\frac{\square}{3} = \frac{4}{12}$

h. $\frac{5}{6} = \frac{\square}{48}$

k. $\frac{\square}{2} = \frac{5}{10}$

l. $\frac{3}{5} = \frac{12}{\square}$

m. $\frac{2}{9} = \frac{\square}{18}$

n. $\frac{8}{\square} = \frac{24}{39}$

o. $\frac{2}{5} = \frac{10}{\square}$

p. $\frac{1}{5} = \frac{5}{\square}$

Lab Activity

Materials required: A cardboard, 8 strips of paper of same size.

Make fraction strips as shown in the figure below. Paste them on the card board.

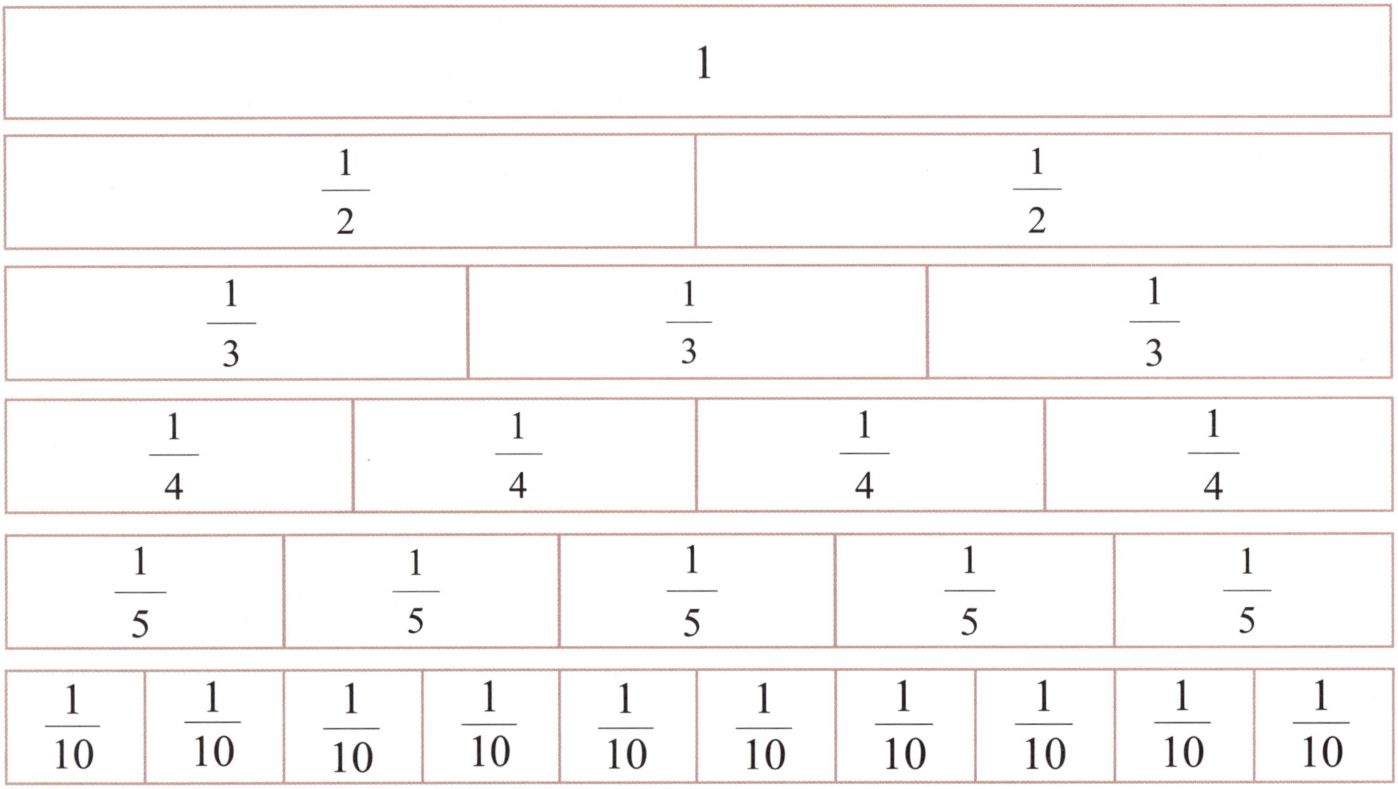

1									
$\frac{1}{2}$					$\frac{1}{2}$				
$\frac{1}{3}$			$\frac{1}{3}$				$\frac{1}{3}$		
$\frac{1}{4}$			$\frac{1}{4}$			$\frac{1}{4}$			$\frac{1}{4}$
$\frac{1}{5}$		$\frac{1}{5}$		$\frac{1}{5}$		$\frac{1}{5}$		$\frac{1}{5}$	
$\frac{1}{10}$	$\frac{1}{10}$	$\frac{1}{10}$	$\frac{1}{10}$	$\frac{1}{10}$	$\frac{1}{10}$	$\frac{1}{10}$	$\frac{1}{10}$	$\frac{1}{10}$	$\frac{1}{10}$

This helps students to understand how many halves, one thirds, one fourths, one fifths etc make a whole.

It can also be used to compare fractions (though it will be taken up in the next grade)

1. Circle the correct answer (use fraction strips as shown above).

a.	How many halves make a whole?	1	2	3
b.	How many one thirds make a whole?	2	3	4
c.	How many one fourths make whole?	1	2	4
d.	How many one fourths make a half?	1	2	4
e.	How many one tenths make a half?	1	5	10
f.	How many one tenths make one fifth?	1	2	5

Mental Maths

1. Tick (✓) the correct answer

   a. What fraction of the letters are vowels in the word 'STUDENT' ?

   (i) $\frac{2}{5}$ ☐ (ii) $\frac{2}{7}$ ☐ (iii) $\frac{5}{3}$ ☐ (iv) $\frac{5}{8}$ ☐

   b. Fraction equivalent is 1/4 is

   (i) $\frac{2}{4}$ ☐ (ii) $\frac{2}{8}$ ☐ (iii) $\frac{3}{4}$ ☐ (iv) $\frac{3}{8}$ ☐

2. Fill in the boxes

   a. $\frac{5}{8} = \frac{\square}{40}$ b. $\frac{21}{56} = \frac{3}{\square}$ c. $\frac{19}{20} = \frac{\square}{60}$

   d. $\frac{17}{34} = \frac{\square}{2}$ e. $\frac{10}{50} = \frac{\square}{500}$ f. $\frac{3}{\square} = \frac{33}{55}$

3. Circle the equivalent fractions in the group

   a. $\frac{8}{24}$ $\frac{7}{14}$ $\frac{1}{2}$ $\frac{2}{10}$ $\frac{18}{180}$

   b. $\frac{11}{111}$ $\frac{10}{100}$ $\frac{100}{200}$ $\frac{4}{8}$ $\frac{3}{6}$

   c. $\frac{2}{6}$ $\frac{4}{12}$ $\frac{19}{95}$ $\frac{6}{18}$ $\frac{3}{15}$

Geometry

9

Let's recall the shapes you have learnt in your previous classes. Identify the following.

Every object around us has a shape or a combination of shapes.

Shapes are formed by straight lines or curved lines.

Point

A dot drawn on the blackboard or floor or your note book is known as a point. Every point has to be given a name. For this we use the letters of the English alphabet A, B, C' D'

A point is like a 'full stop'. It has no thickness.

Line

A line is a collection of points. In a line more and more points keep joining in on both sides. So, it is said a line extends endlessly (indefinitely) on both sides.

A line has no end points. Since it is made up of points, which have no breadth, a line has no breadth.

Representation of a line

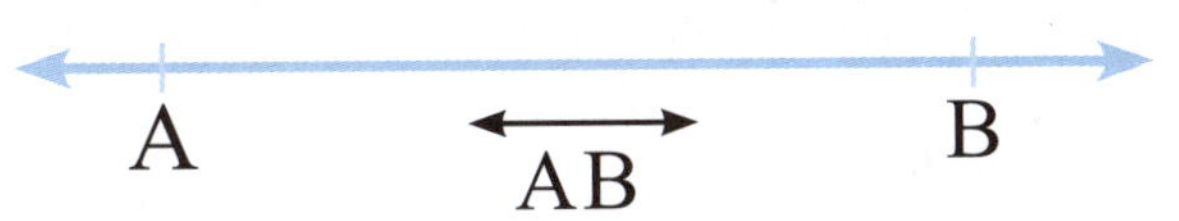

$\overleftrightarrow{AB}$

Two arrowheads on either side indicating it extends on both sides.

It is named by any two points on it.

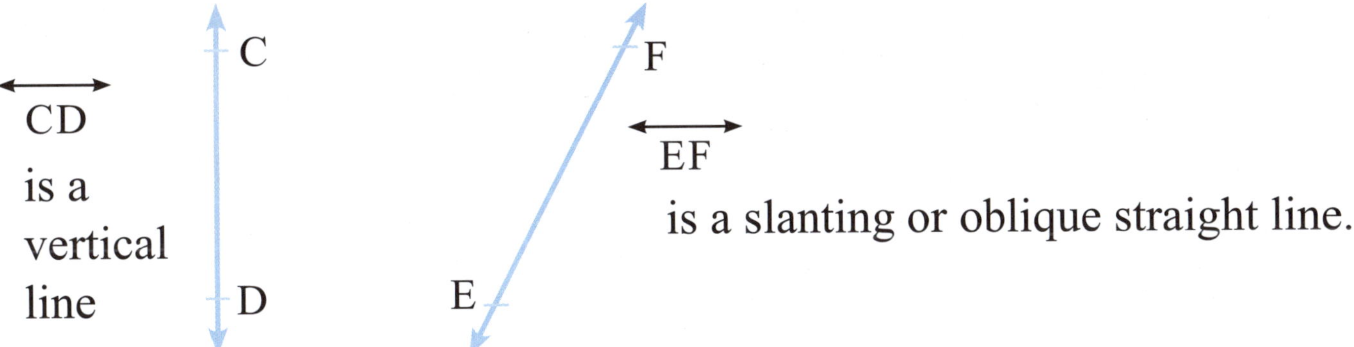

$\overleftrightarrow{CD}$ is a vertical line

$\overleftrightarrow{EF}$ is a slanting or oblique straight line.

Line segment

A line segment is a part of the line. It has a fixed length and two end points.

$\overline{PQ}$ is a line segment of length 4 cm.

Line segments can also be horizontal, vertical or slanting.

Ray

A ray starts from an end point and can extend in one direction only. It cannot be measured.

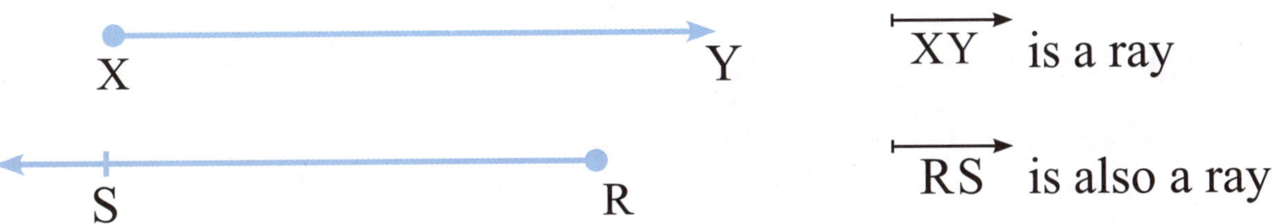

$\overrightarrow{XY}$ is a ray

$\overrightarrow{RS}$ is also a ray

Measuring line segments

Take a scale. Keep the o mark of the scale at one end point of the line segment and read the other end point on the scale.

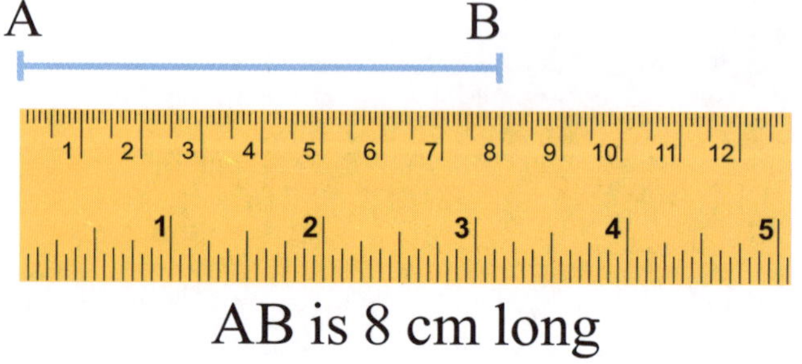

AB is 8 cm long

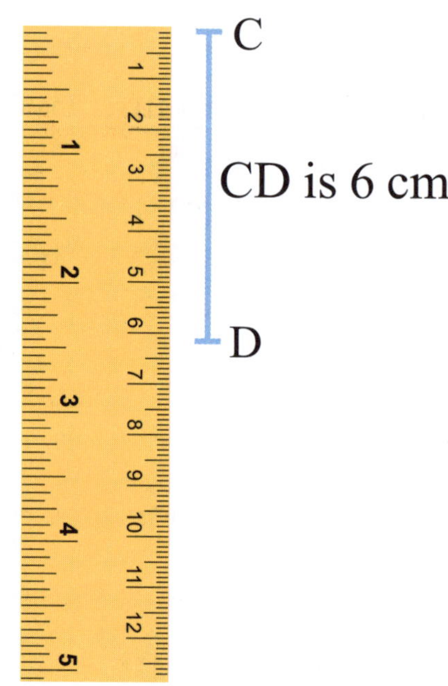

CD is 6 cm

Drawing a line segment

Materials required: A scale, a well sharpened pencil

Aim: Draw a line segment of length 4 cm

Method:

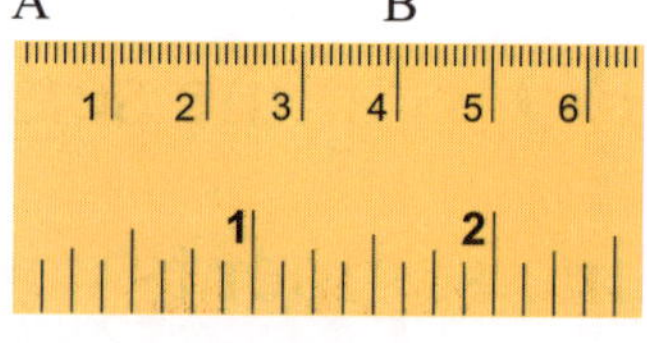

1. Mark a point A on paper
2. Keep the scale with o mark at A
3. Now see the 4 cm mark on scale and mark point B at that point.
4. Join AB along the edge of the scale
5. AB is the required line segment

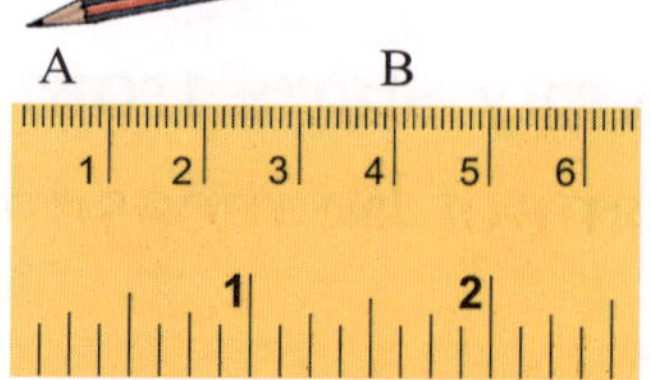

While drawing line segments the pencil should be well sharpened, scale should be held firmly and lines should not be very dark

Exercise 9.1

1. Measure the line segments and write length in cm.

a. F G

b. M N

c. P Q

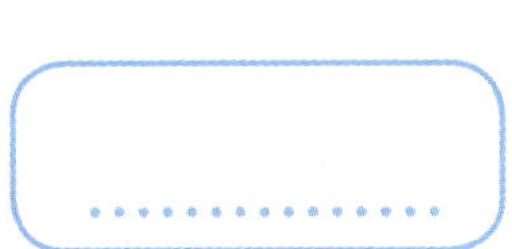

d.

2. Draw line segments of the following measurements and name them.

   a. 5 cm

   b. 8 cm

   c. 2 cm

   d. 10 cm

3. Name the line segments in each figure and mention the points at which the line segments meet.

a.

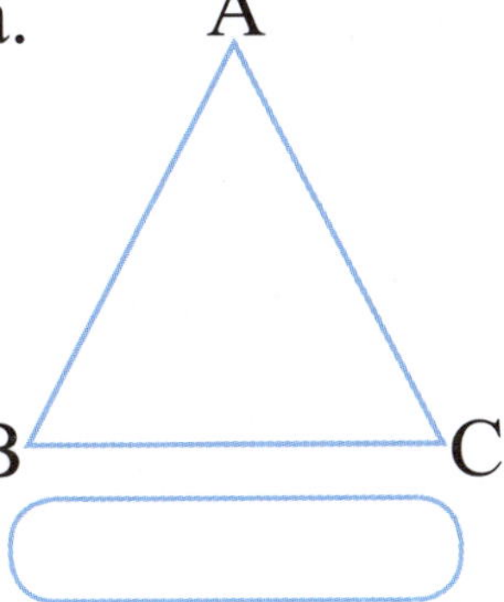

b.

c.

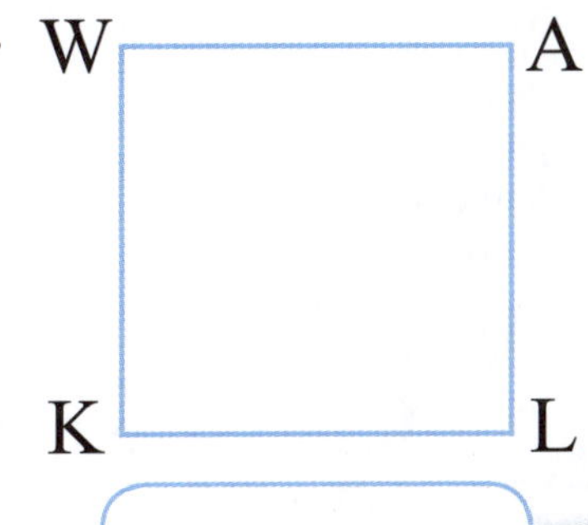

4. Measure the length of the following objects with a scale.
   a. Your note book (length)
   b. Your Maths book (length)
   c. A pencil
   d. A crayon
   e. A chalk
   f. An eraser

Perimeter

Rajesh started measuring the sides of his books, note books, pencil boxes.

He measured the sides of his Maths book. He found it was 27 cm long and 21 cm wide. He measured the other two sides and found them to be same.

So, he added the 4 sides and found 27 cm + 21 cm + 27 cm + 21 = 96 cm

This length along the edges (or boundary) of the book is called perimeter of the book. All closed figures have perimeter.

Perimeter can also be the distance around a figure. Perimeter is the sum of the lengths of the sides of the figure.

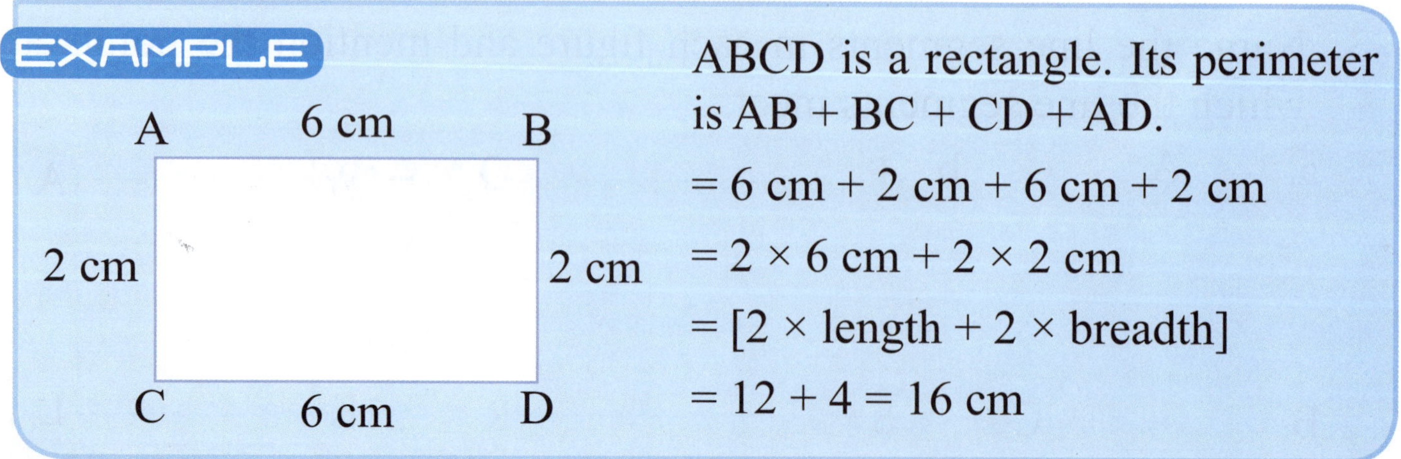

ABCD is a rectangle. Its perimeter is AB + BC + CD + AD.

= 6 cm + 2 cm + 6 cm + 2 cm

= 2 × 6 cm + 2 × 2 cm

= [2 × length + 2 × breadth]

= 12 + 4 = 16 cm

EXAMPLE

P 4 cm Q

7 cm 7 cm

S 4 cm R

Find the perimeter of PQRS

We can write

Perimeter of PQRS = 2 length + 2 breadth

= 2 × 7 cm + 2 × 4cm

= 14 cm + 8 cm

= 22 cm.

You can verify by adding all the 4 sides.

7 cm + 4 cm + 7 cm + 4 cm = 22 cm

Perimeter of a rectangle = 2 × length + 2 × breadth

Perimeter of a square

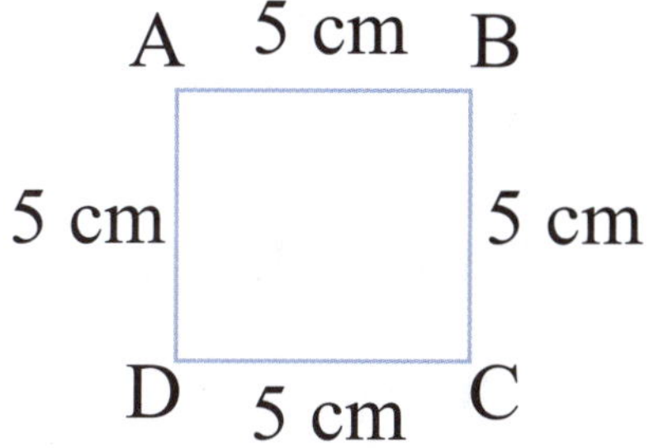

All the sides of a square are equal. Its perimeter

= 5 cm + 5 cm + 5 cm + 5 cm = 20 cm

= or 4 × 5 cm

= 20 cm

Perimeter of a square = sum of its 4 sides or 4 × length of the sides

Perimeter of a triangle

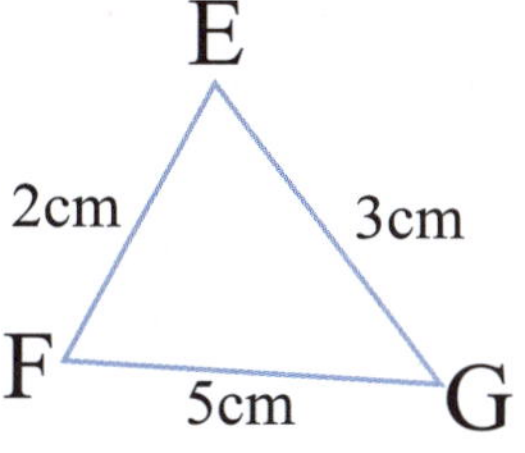

Perimeter of EFG

= EF + FG + EG

= 2 cm + 5 cm + 3 cm

= 10 cm

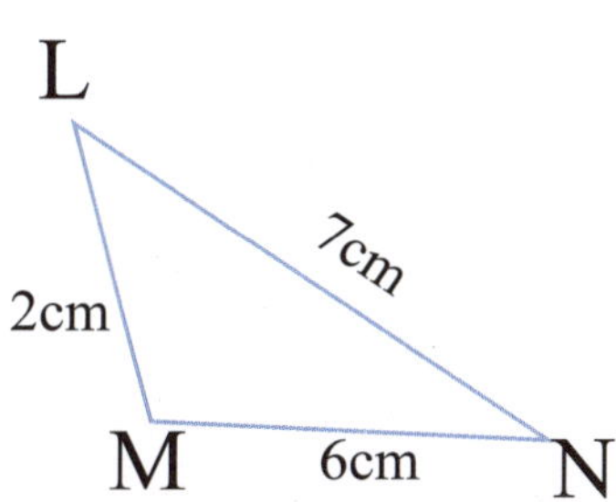

Perimeter of LMN

= MN + LN + LM

= 6 cm + 7 cm + 4 cm

= 17 cm

Perimeter of a triangle = sum of all sides of the triangle

Perimeter of other figures

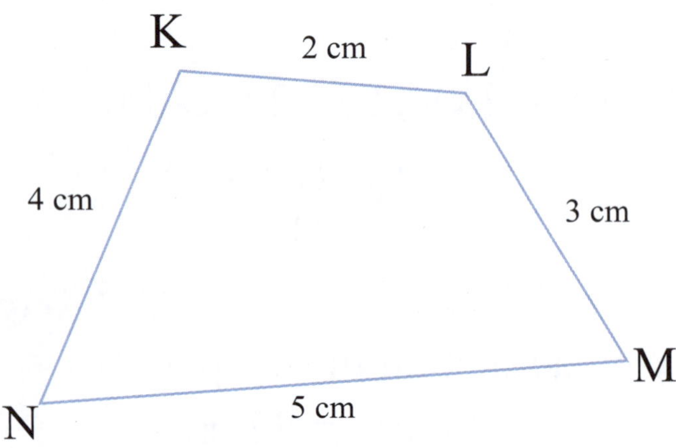

Perimeter is length of the boundary.

Perimeter of a polygon = Sum of all the sides of the polygon

Perimeter of KLMN

= KL + LM + MN + NK

= 2 + 3 + 5 + 4

= 14 cm

Exercise 9.2

1. Find the perimeter of the following figures.

a. 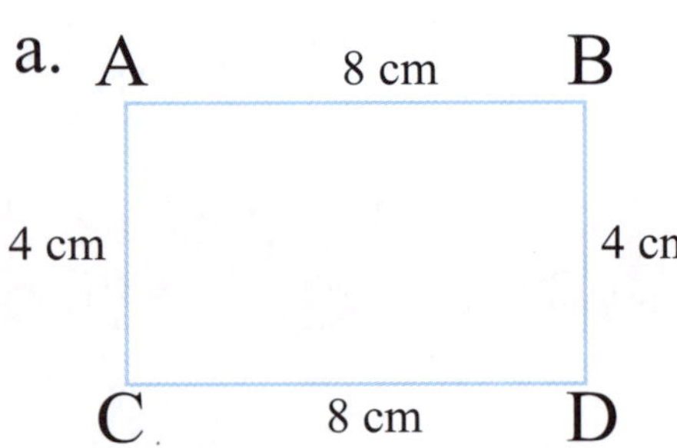

b. 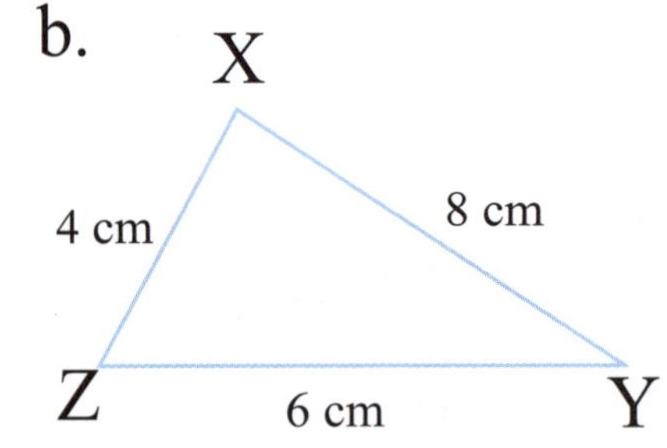

c. 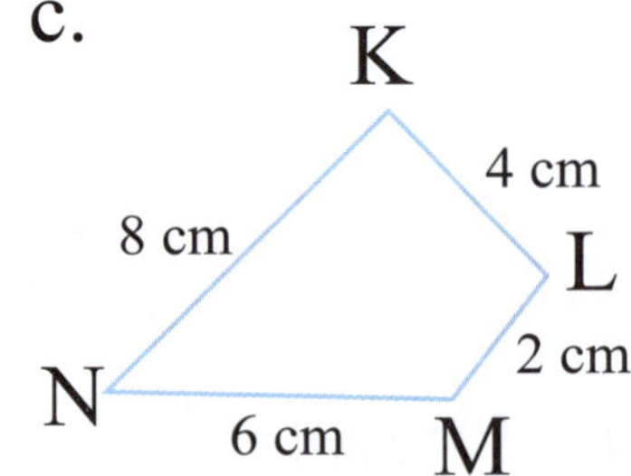

2. Find the perimeters of squares whose one side is

a. 5 cm b. 8 cm c. 2 cm d. 10 cm

3. Which figure has greater perimeter (a) or (b)?

a. 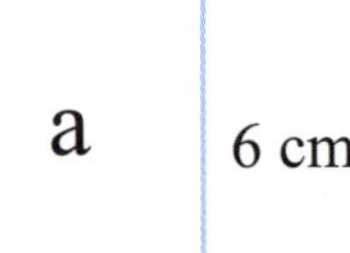

b. 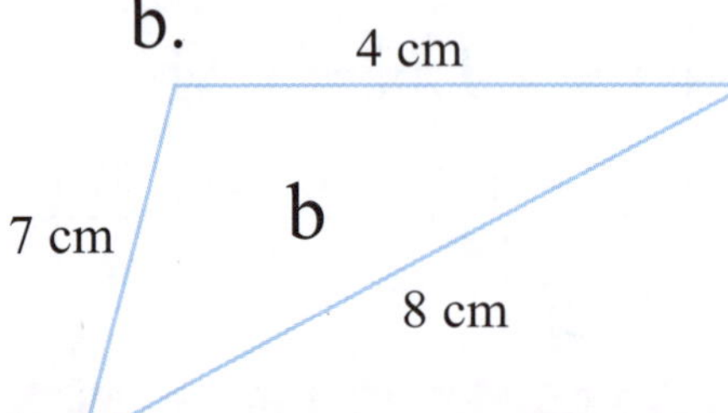

4. Find the missing length of the side. The perimeter is written inside the figure.

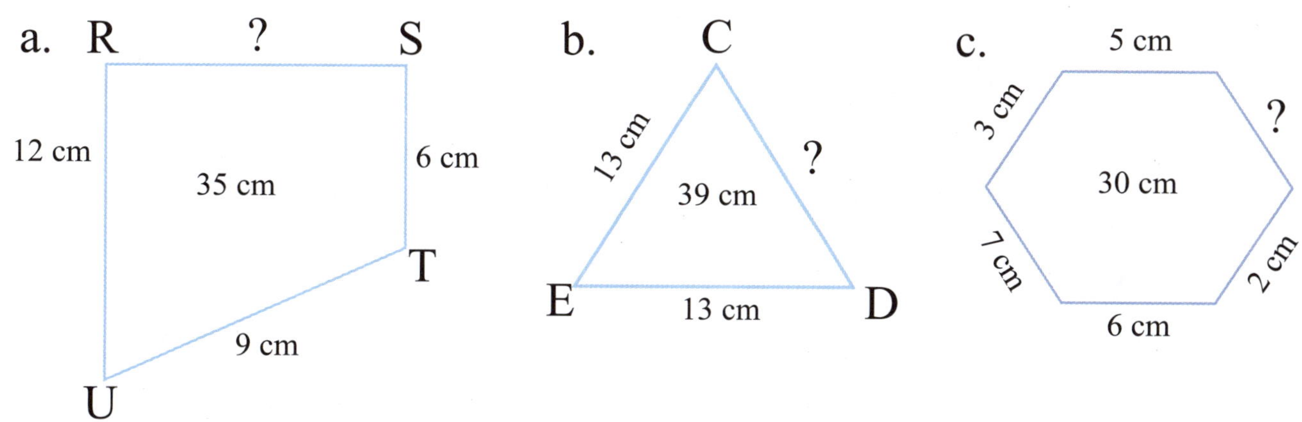

5. Each square has a side of 1cm, find the perimeters of the figures.

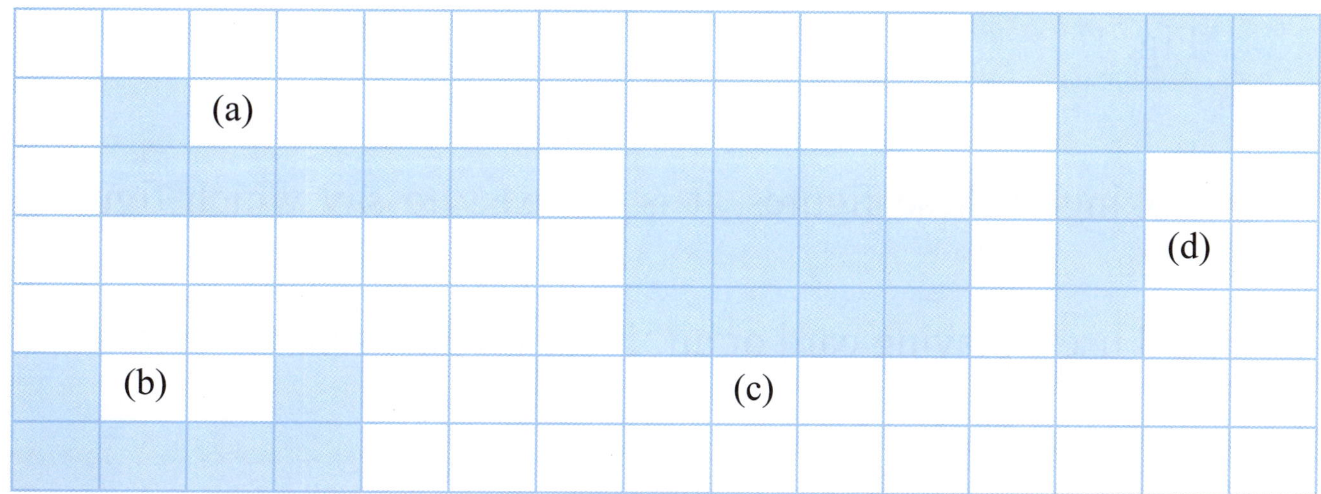

Area

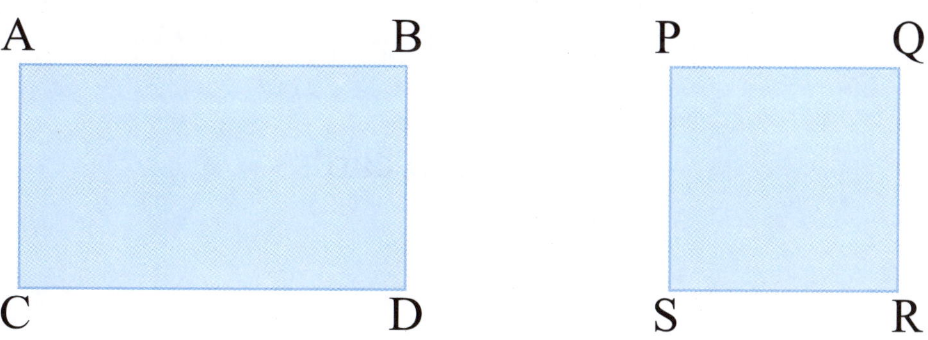

The shaded portion is the area covered by the rectangle and the square.

Here area of rectangle seems to be more than area of square

A closed figure covers some surface and this is its area.

Fig. 1 Fig. 2

Now looking at these figures, it is not easy to say which figure has a larger area.

We could use a playing card or an 'I' card to measure the area.

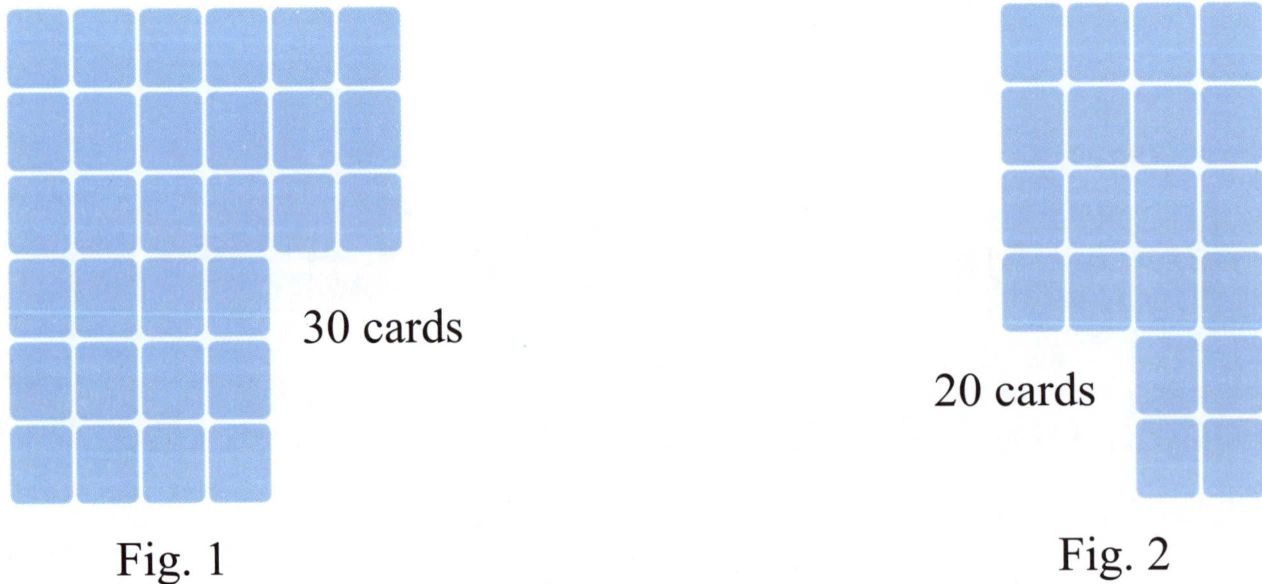

Fig. 1 Fig. 2

So, figure 1 has greater area.

Lab Activity

Use playing cards to cover the surface of your (1) Notebook (2) Maths book (3) English book

Unit of Area

Fig 1 = 12 squares

Fig 2 = 7 squares

The area of 1 square of side 1 cm is 1 square cm (or sq cm)

So, area of Fig 1 is 12 sq cm as it is 12 squares and area of each square is 1 sq cm.

Area of Fig 2 = 7 sq cm.

Exercise 9.3

1. By counting the number of unit squares, find the areas of the following rectangles and squares.

a.

Area = ____ sq cm

b.

Area = ____ sq cm

c.

Area = ____ sq cm

d.

Area = ____ sq cm

2. Find areas of following figures. The squares have sides 1 cm.

Area =

4

Area = 1

2

Area =

Area =

3 Area =

5

Circles

Circle is a closed figure. It is a shape made by a curved line.

Drawing Circles

A bottle cap, a coin, top of a glass, bangle can he put on a sheet of paper. When the outline is drawn with a pencil, we get a circle.

A pencil drawing the boundary of a Glass, a coin

A compass helps us draw circles of any size (big or small)

Centre of a circle

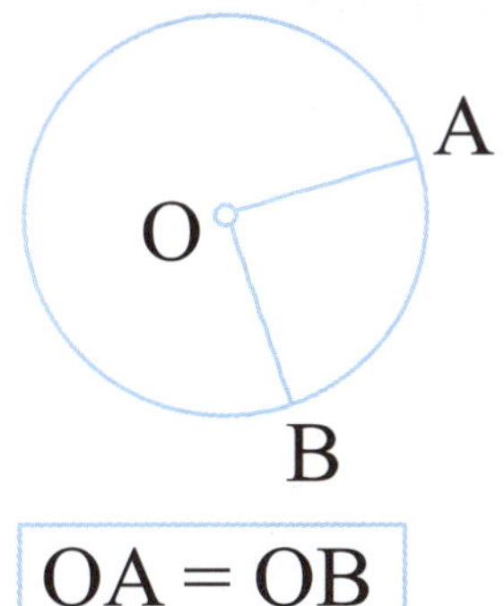

OA = OB

A fixed point inside the circle. The point on which the needle of the compass is kept, to draw a circles its centre O is centre. Every point on the circle is at an equal distance from the centre. A and B are points on the circle.

Radius: OA is the radius of the circle.

OA = OB

Radius of circle is fixed. It does not change.

Radius is the fixed distance between the centre of the circle and any point on the circle.

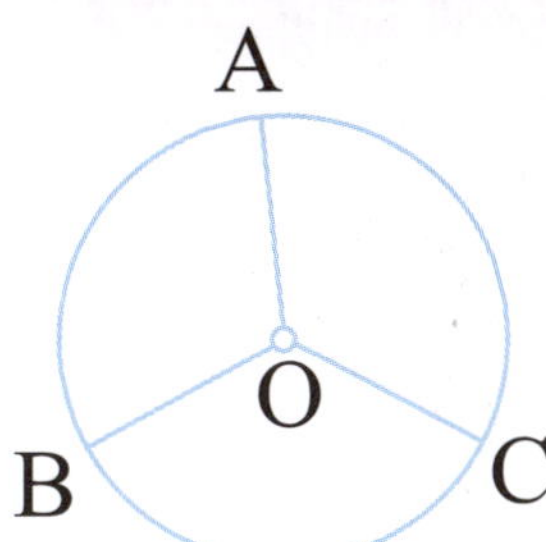

OA, OB, OC are radii

(1 radius, two radii)

How many radii can a circle have?

Chord of a circle

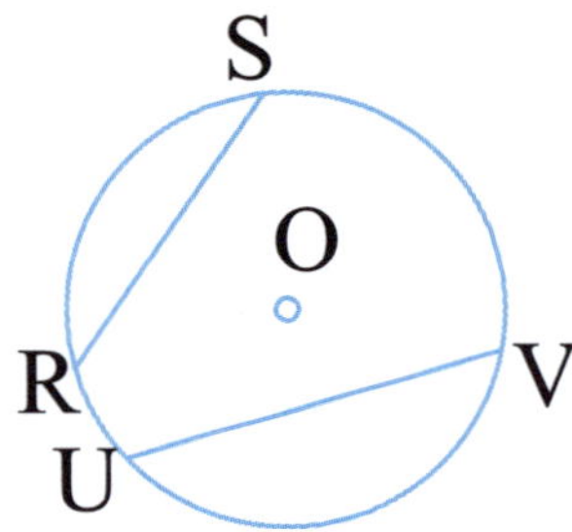

If any two points on a circle are joined, we get a line segment. It is called a chord of the circle RS and UV are chords of the circle. A circle has many chords. Different chords can be of different lengths.

Diameter

A chord of a circle, that passes through the centre, is called the diameter of the circle.

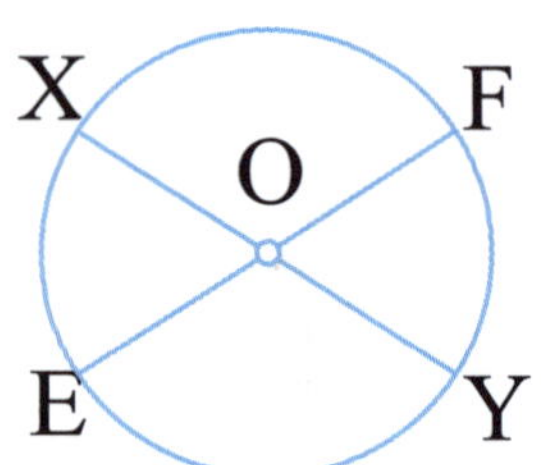

XY and EF are diameters of the circle.

A circle has many diameters and all diameters are of same length.

Length of EF = length of XY

Draw a circle of radius 3cm

EF = 6 cm, OE = 3 cm

Diameter = 2 × 3

= 2 × radius

A diameter is also a chord.

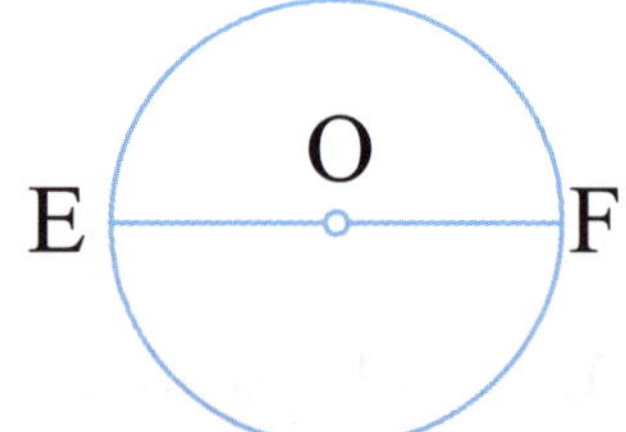

All diameters are chords
But all chords are not diameters.

A circle has many chords, radii, diameters. But only one centre

Exercise 9.4

1. See each figure and fill in the blanks.

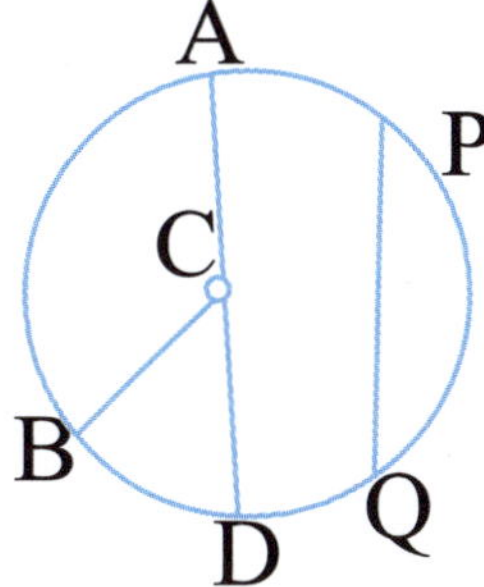

a. Name the centre ____________

(i) 3 radii ____________

(ii) A chord ____________

(iii) A diameter ____________

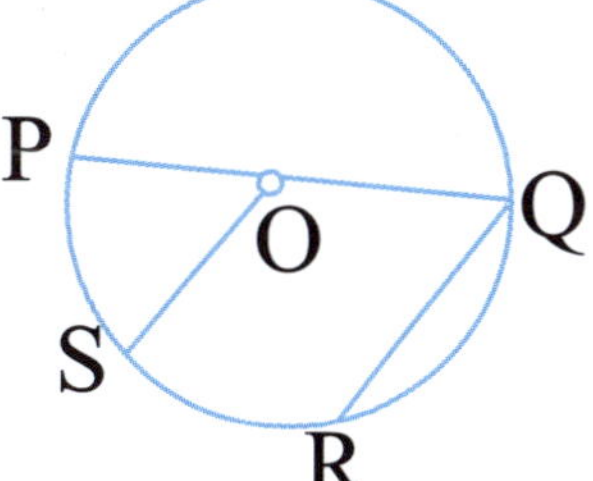

b. Name the centre ____________

(i) 2 radii ____________

(ii) 1 diameter ____________

(iii) 1 chord ____________

2. In the given figures draw the following.

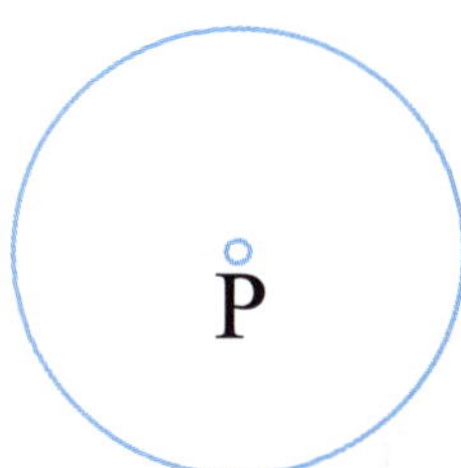

A radius PM

A chord AB

A diameter SQ

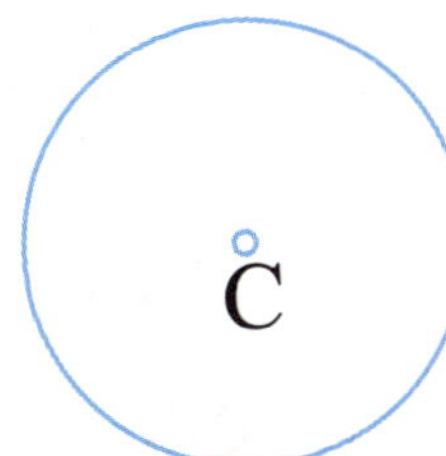

A radius CN

A chord YZ

A diameter MN

3. Draw a diameter and write the measurements in the blank space.

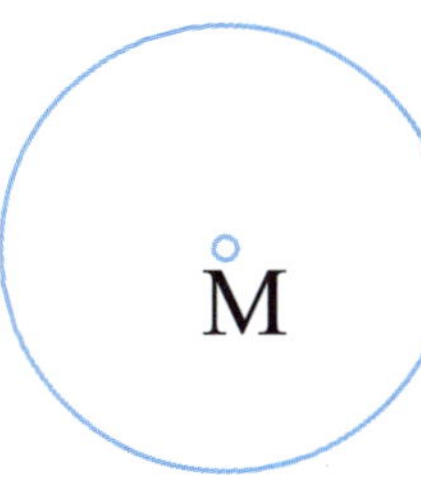

Name it

Diameter = ______cm

Radius = ______cm

4. Radii of circles are given. Find their diameters.

   a. 10 cm

   b. 6 cm

   c. 17 cm

   d. 100 cm

5. Diameters of circles are given. Find the radius of each.

   a. 16 cm

   b. 22 cm

   c. 50 cm

   d. 8 cm

6. Diameter of a wheel is 1 m. find its radius.

7. Radius of a coin is 3 cm. Find its diameter.

Activity on circles

Take a bangle. Draw its outline on a paper. Cut out the circle.
Find its centre by folding it along 2 diameters.

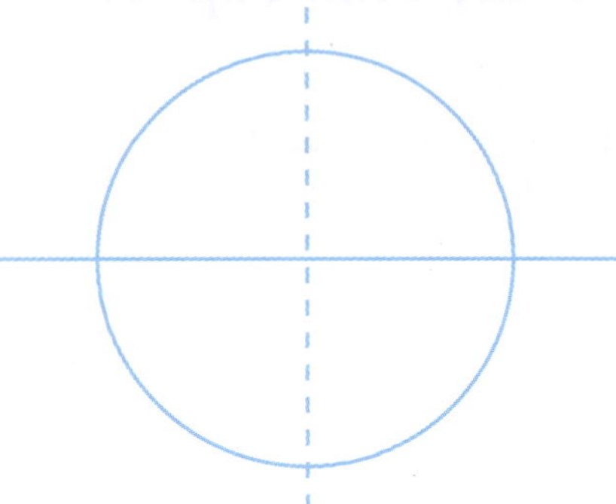

Find the radius.

Find the diameter.

2. Use a compass for creating different patterns in a circle.

Activity

Circle: How to find the centre

Put a glass upside down an a sheet of paper and trace the outer surface with a pencil.

The shape is the circle. We could use a bangle also to get a circle.

Cut out the circle. Fold it twice to get 4 equal parts.

The point at which the two creases meet is the centre. Name it O

The distance from O to A is a radius.

OA, DB, OC, OD are the radius.

In fig (ii) we can see OD falls on OD.

So, OB = OD

Similarly OA = OC. Fold it further along dotted Line and see

OC = OD.

BD the diameter = OB + OD = 2 OB

Symmetry

10

If you fold along the dotted line, one part will exactly fit over the other part. Such figures are called **symmetrical figures**. The line is called the **line of symmetry**. Are all figures symmetrical?

No, there are lots of figures which are not symmetrical.

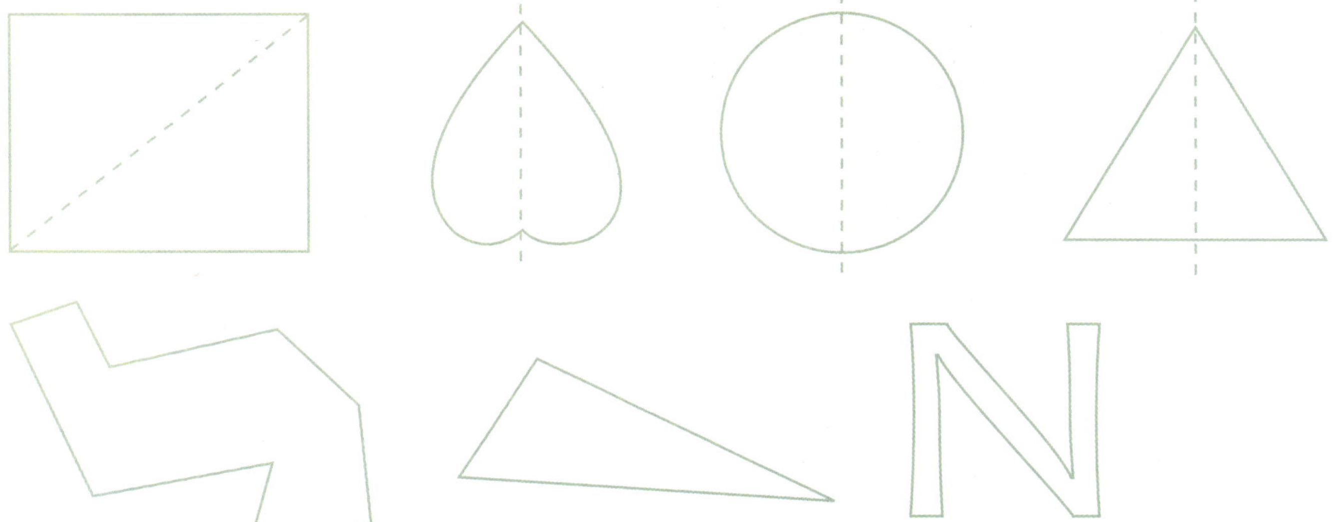

Some figures have more than one line of symmetry.

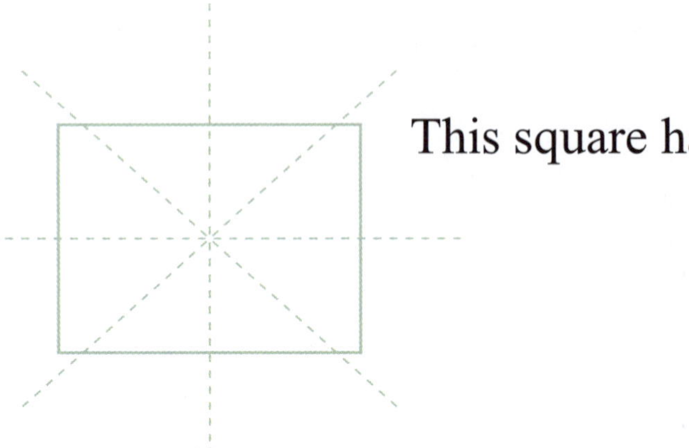

This square has four lines of symmetry.

This figure has two lines of symmetry

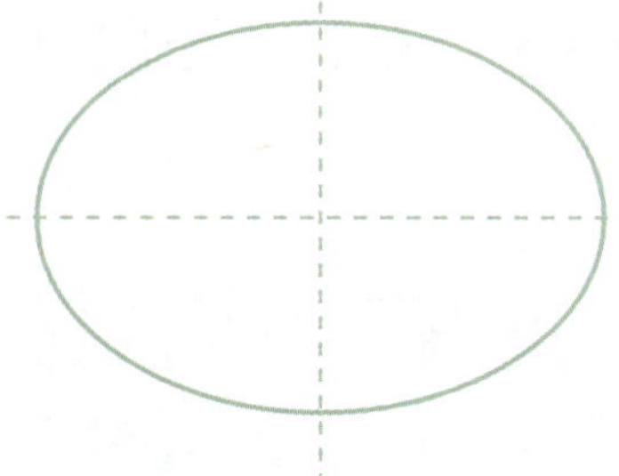

Lab Activity

Symmetry

Materials required: Rectangular sheets of paper, square sheets of paper.

Method: Divide students into groups of 4. Each group should be given 2 rectangular and 2 square sheets.

a. Let them find the line of symmetry by folding.

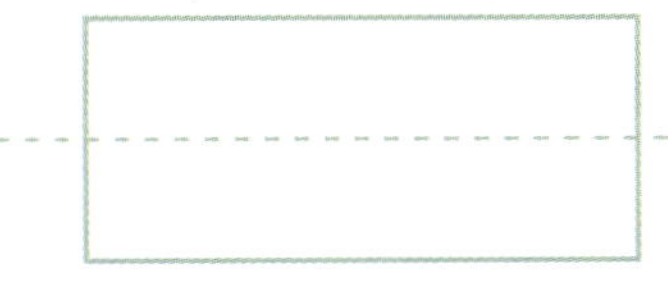

One is the dotted line. Fold along this line and you will see the two parts cover each other exactly. Are these lines of symmetry? Check it out.

 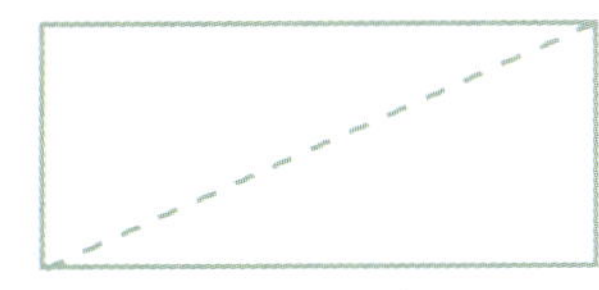 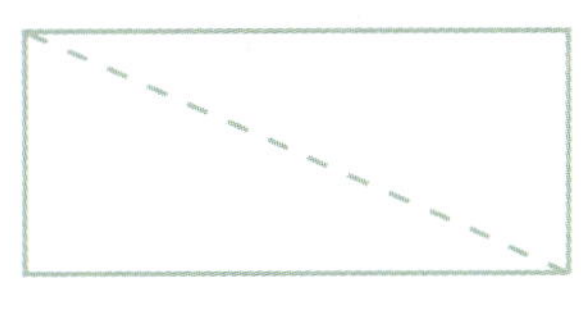 

How many axis of symmetry does a rectangle have 2 or 4?

Answer ....

b. Take a square piece and do the same.

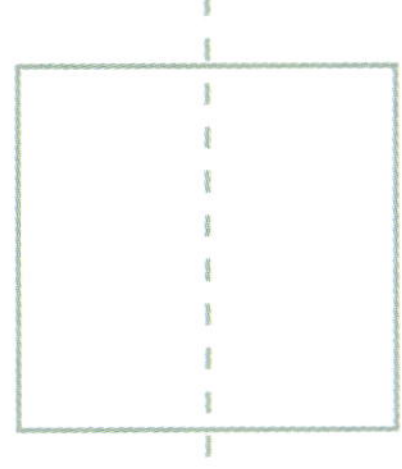 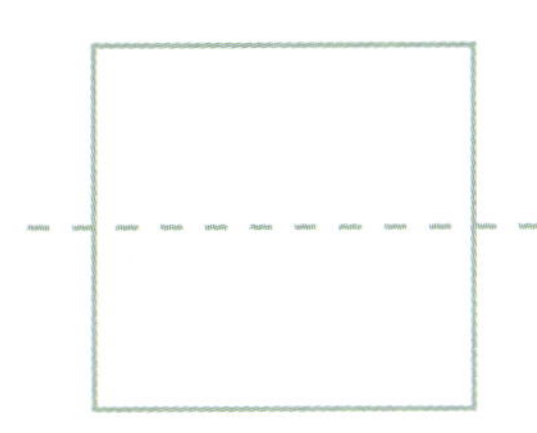 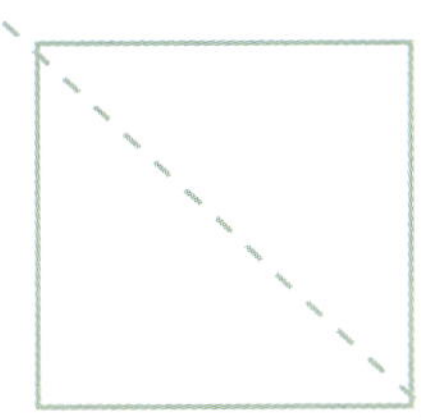 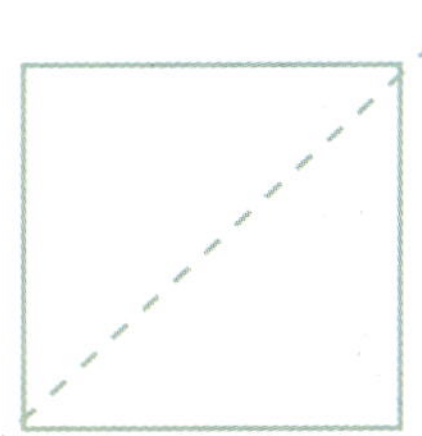

Take cut outs of circles. Fold along diameters. How many lines of symmetry can a circle have?

Common Solid Shapes

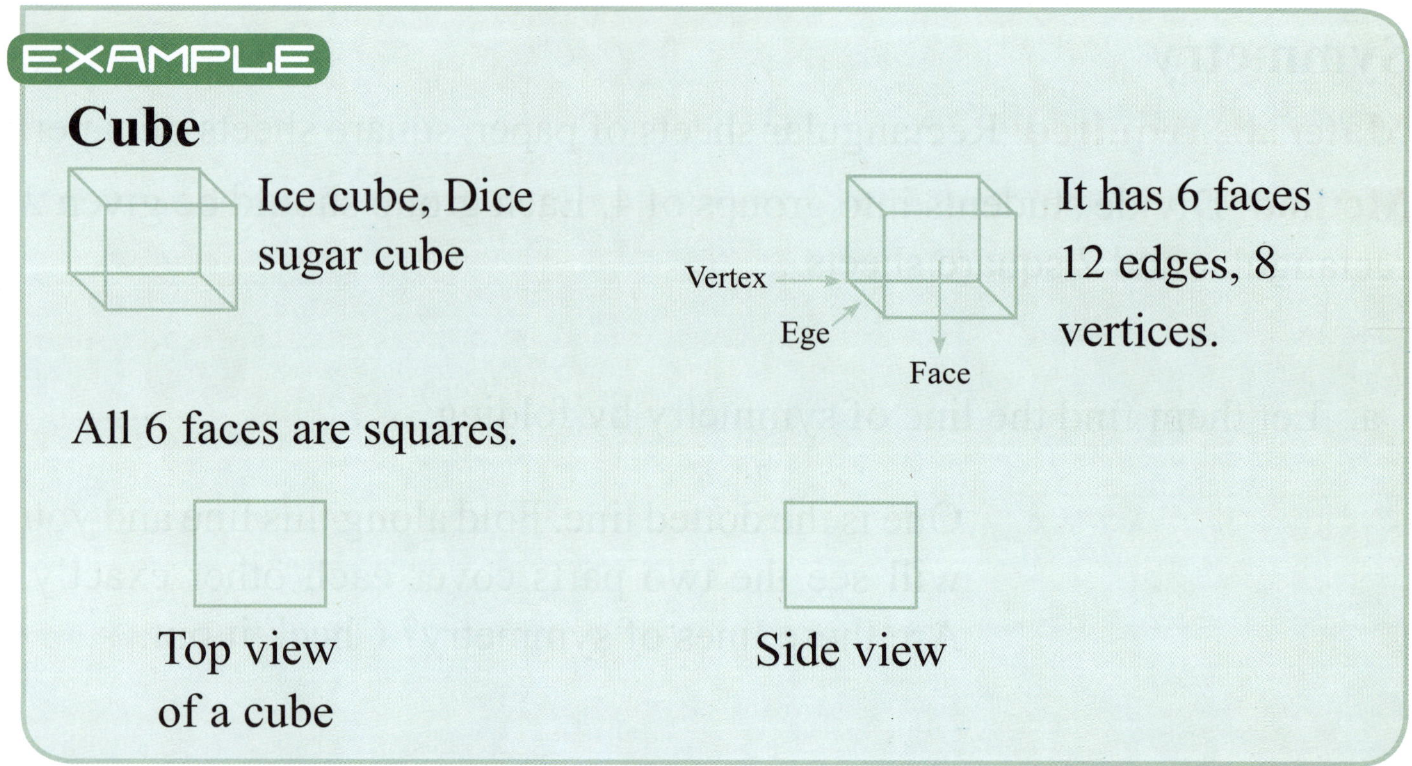

Let us view different objects from top, and the side and fill in the table below.

Object	Top view	Side view

Symmetry

When we look in the mirror, our image is formed.

Look at the figures given. The dotted line is the line of the mirror.

These are examples of reflection.

Look at the following figures.

Are these reflections?

No, they are not.

The second figure is obtained by rotating the first figure.

Exercise 10.1

1. Put a (✓) tick on the figures which are symmetrical.

a. 

b. 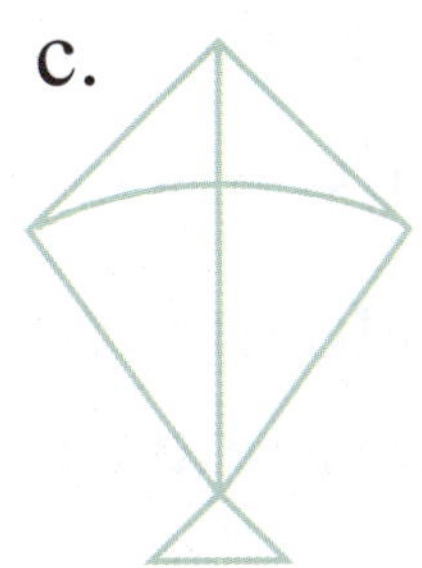

c. 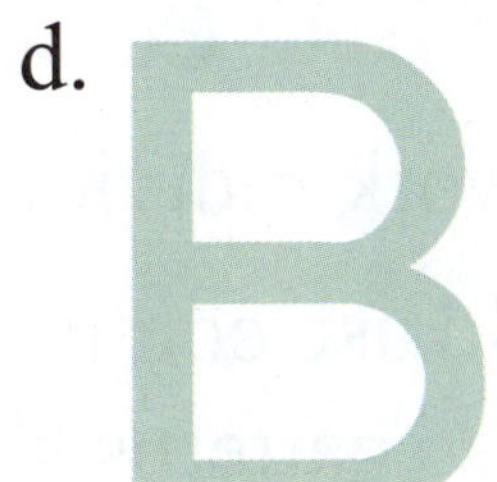

d. 

e.

2. Is the dotted line the line of symmetry? Write [Y] for yes and [N] for no.

a. 

b. 

c. 

d. 

3. Draw the line of symmetry in the following

a. 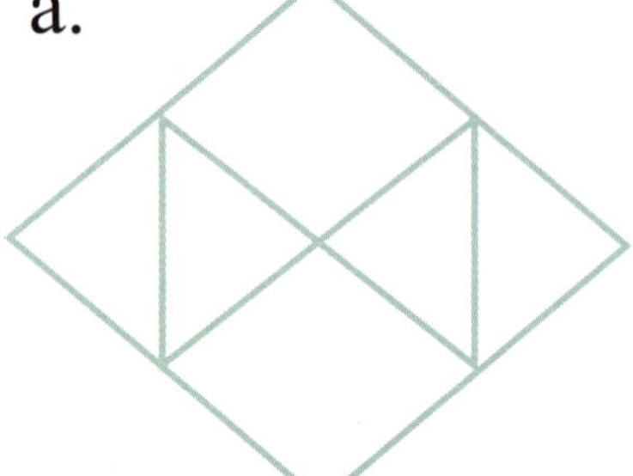

b. 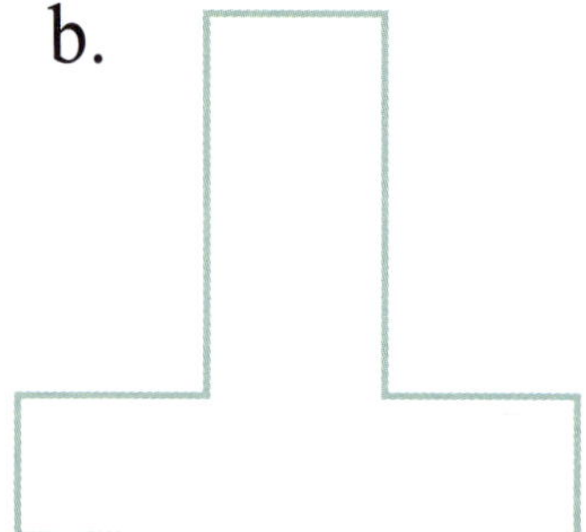

c. 

d. 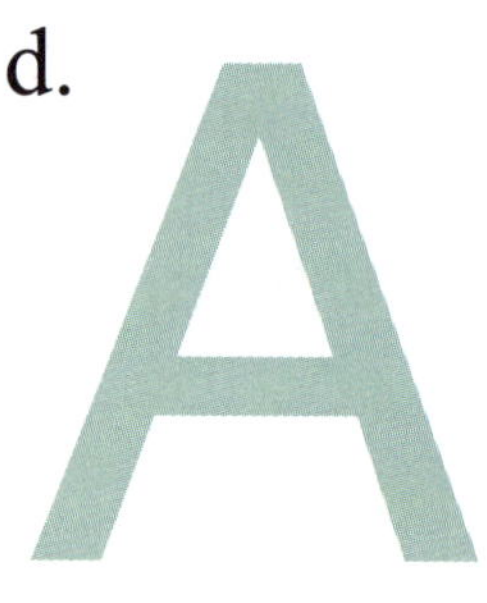

4. Are the figures reflections?

a. 

b. 

c.

EXAMPLE

Symmetry

Materials required: Compass, pencil, colours sheets of papers.

Students can work individually.

Students should use compass to make various patterns. They should colour and these patterns should be displayed.

Measurement of Weight (mass), Capacity and Length

11

Commonly used units for weight or mass are grams and kilograms

1000 g = 1 kg

6000 g = 6 kg

500 g + 500 g = 1kg.

1/2 kg = 500 g

The standard weights are like this

We weigh something using a balance. On one side a pan standard weight is kept and on the other, the object to be weighed.

If weights are equal, pans balance. The pan with heavier weight goes down.

Sometimes a weighing scale is also used. A weighing scale has a dial where weight can be read.

Exercise 11.1

1. Write the correct weights so that the weights balance.

a. ⬡ + ⬡ + ⬡ = ⬡ + ⬡

2 kg   500 g   500 g   ____kg   ____kg

b. ⬡ = ⬡ + ⬡ + ⬡ + ⬡ + ⬡

1 kg   ____g   ____g   ____g   ____g   ____g

c. ⬡ + ⬡ + ⬡ + ⬡ = ⬡ + ⬡

500 g 500 g 500 g 500 g ___kg ___kg

d. ⬡ + ⬡ = ⬡ + ⬡ + ⬡

1 kg 1 kg ____kg ____g ____g

2. In Rahim's fresh fruit stall

a. Find the cost of :

(i) 2 kg pears __________

(ii) 3 pineapples __________

(iii) 1 kg 500 g mangoes __________

(iv) 1 kg oranges & 1 pineapple __________

(v) 2 dozen bananas __________

(vi) 1 doz bananas, __________

(vii) 2 kg oranges, 2 pineapples __________

Exercise 11.2

1. Usha bought 1 kg of kiwis. She had bags that could carry 200 g only. How many bags would she need?
2. A shopkeeper packed fruits in 500 g packets. How many packets would he give to someone who buys.

	Weight	No. of packets
a.	1 kg	______________
b.	2 kg	______________
c.	2 1/2 kg	______________
d.	1 1/2 kg	______________

3. A man bought 2 ½ kg potatoes, 1½ kg onions, ¼ kg peas, ½ kg tomatoes, 3 kg mutton.

   a. Potatoes __________g

   b. Peas __________g

   c. Onions__________g

   d. Tomatoes __________g

   e. Mutton__________g

Addition and subtraction

1. Add 32 kg 435 g and 248 kg 687 g

Kg	g
1 1	1 1
3 2	4 3 5
+2 4 8	+6 8 7
2 8 1	1 2 2

Answer: 281 kg 122 g

2. Find the difference 265 kg 200 g 354 kg

Kg	g
2 4 3	
3 5 4	1 0 0 0
−2 6 5	−2 0 0
8 8	8 0 0

0 < 200 so, borrow 1 kg = 1000 g from 354 kg

Answer: 88 kg 800 g

Exercise 11.3

1. Anil has lost weight. Earlier he was 51 kg now he is 48 kg 500 g. How much weight has he lost?
2. A sack had 90 kg of rice. On Monday 23 kg 575 g was taken out and on Tuesday 28 kg 650 g. How much rice was left in the bag?

Measurement of Capacity

Capacity of a container is the amount of liquid it can hold.

Let us see recall what we learnt in the previous classes.

Exercise 11.4

1. Convert into ml

   a. 10l

   b. 14l

   c. 25l 250 ml

   d. 5l 990 ml

2. Convert into l

   a. 8000 ml

   b. 3805 ml = ______ l __________ ml

   c. 26420 ml = ______ l __________ ml

   d. 4875 ml = ______ l __________ ml

3. A bucket contains 8 l of water. How many jugs of capacity 500 ml can be filled from it?

4. 4 packets of 250 ml of juice is poured into a container. How much of juice is in the container?

Addition and subtraction

1. Find the sum 27 l 315 ml, 16 l 450 ml, 248 l, 5 ml

L	ml
²27	3¹15
+16	450
+248	005
291	770

Answer: 2911 770 ml

2. Find the difference of 175 l 695 ml and 3001 100 ml

L	ml
2 9 9	9 9 1
~~3~~ ~~0~~ ~~0~~	~~1~~ ~~0~~ ~~0~~ 0
−175	−695
124	305

Answer: 124 l 305 ml

Measurement of length

Fill in the blanks

1. 1 km = ______________ m
2. 4 m = ______________ cm
3. 7 m 20 cm = ______________ cm
4. 6 km 105 m = ______________ m
5. 3500 m = _________ km _________ m
6. 600 cm = ______________ m
7. 1000 cm = ______________ m
8. 826 cm = _________ m _________ cm

Addition and subtraction

1. Add 54 km 275 m, 76 km 550 m and 189 km 9 cm

KM	M
[1]54	275
+76	550
+186	9
319	834

Answer: 319 km 834 m

2. Find the difference of 76 m 4 cm and 29 m 55 cm

m	cm
6 15	9 14
~~7~~~~6~~	1~~0~~~~4~~
−29	−55
46	49

Answer: 46 m 49 cm

Exercise 11.5

1. Add

   a. 49 m 38 cm, 85 m 7 cm and 108 m 75 cm

   b. 130 km 450 m, 85 km 666 m and 7 km 35 m

   c. 76 m 2 cm, 80 m 37 cm ; 95 cm

2. Find the difference

   a. 102 km 45 m and 354 km 2 m   b. 406 m 8 cm and 77 m 85 cm

   c. 125 m 5 cm and 98 m 86 cm

3. From a roll of 120 cm long electric wire, two pieces of 25 m 35 cm and 68 m 75 cm are cut. Find the length of wire left in the roll.

4. Distance from Mumbai to Puna is 180 km. Anil travelled 78 km 48 m by bus and the rest by car. How much distance did he cover by car?

Measurement

1. Fill in the blanks with appropriate units.

   a. A bottle of cold drink has 500 __________ of cold drink

   b. The dropper has 3 __________ of medicine

   c. The bucket holds 8 __________ of water

   d. The length of the basketball court is 12 __________.

   e. Height of my water bottle is 25 __________.

   f. My eraser weighs 5 __________.

   g. A tablespoon of salt weighs 5 __________.

   h. My house is 5 __________ from the school.

2. Complete the following.

   a. 500 ml + __________ ml = 1 l

   b. 400 g + __________ g = 1 kg

   c. __________ cm + 40 cm = 1 m

   d. 300 m + __________ m = 1 km

Time

12

Write the time

Draw the hands of the clock to show the time.

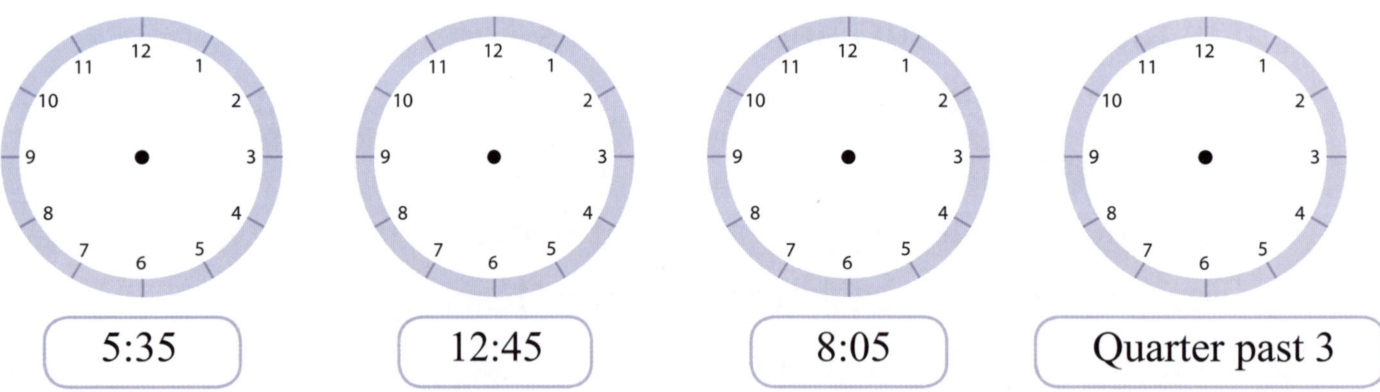

'Quarter to'

We have seen half hour is 30 minutes and quarter hour is 15 minutes.

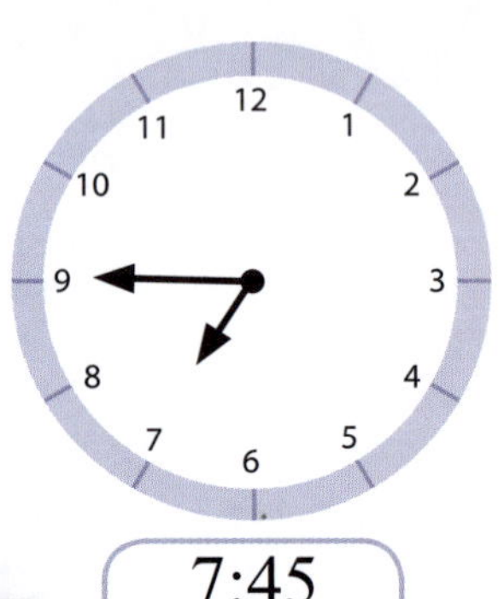

7:45 can be written as

45 minutes past 7.

It is not yet 8 o' clock.

After how many minutes will it be 8 o' clock?

15 mins

So, this can be written as quarter to 8.

EXAMPLE

The time is 3:45 or quarter to 4

After how many minutes will it be 6 o' clock?

5 mins.

The time can be written as 5 minutes to 6.

5 : 55 or 5 minutes to 6

Exercise 12.1

1. Read the time and write in two ways.

a. 

1:50

10 mins to 2

b. 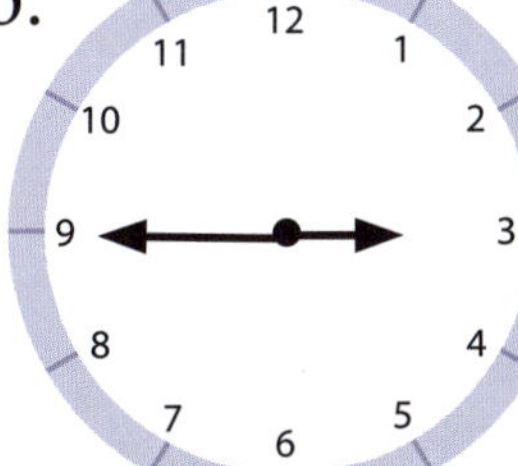

c. 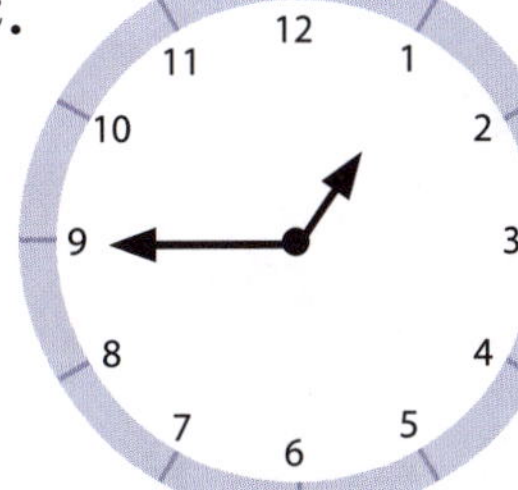

d. 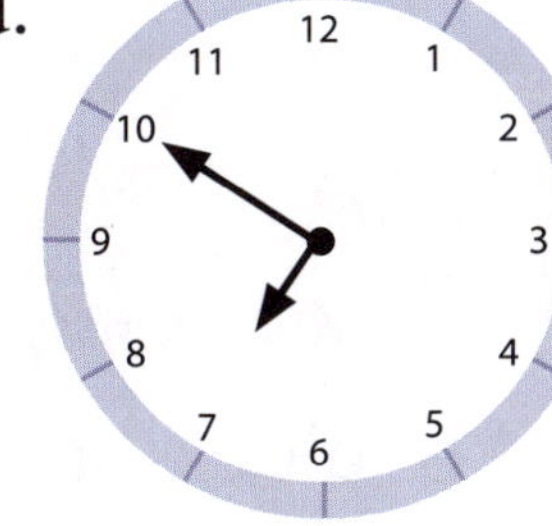

e.

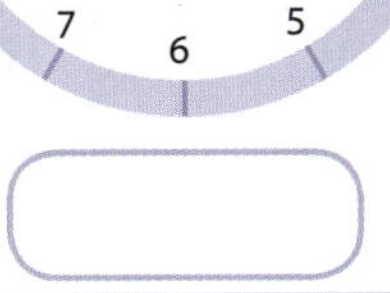

f. 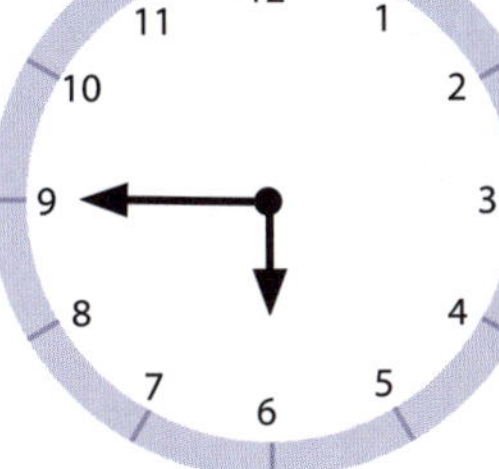

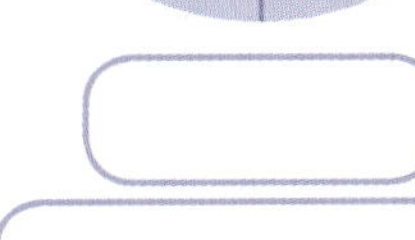

g. 

h. 

A.M. and P. M.

On the clock we see 12 numbers. In one day there are 24 hours. The hour hand of the clock goes round the clock two times.

A friend of mine said his train is arriving at 4 o' cock. I did not know if it was morning or evening.

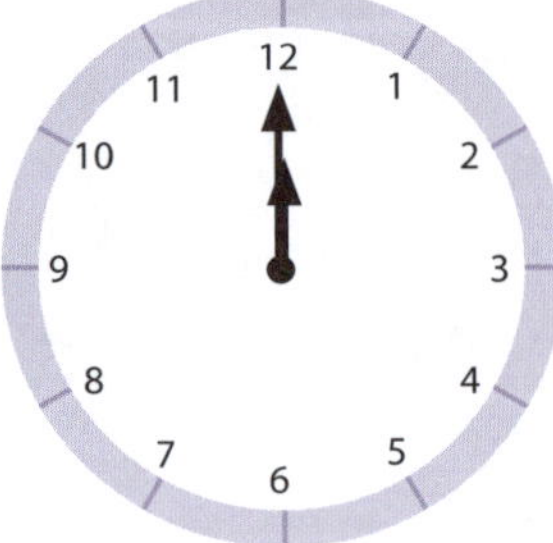

The clock shows 12 o' clock.

But is it 12 noon or 12 midnight?

To remove this confusion, time from

12 midnight to 12 noon is denoted by a. m. (ante meridien)

12 noon to 12 midnight is denoted by p. m. (post meridien)

12 o' clock in the day is 12 noon
12 o' clock at night is 12 midnight

12 o' clock has **no a. m.** or **p. m.** It is 12 noon or 12 midnight

Exercise 12.2

1. Fill in the time with a. m. or p. m.

evening	morning	morning	evening	night
5.00 p.m	5 ____	7:30 ____	6 ____	10:30 ____

2. What is the time? (a.m. / p.m.)

a. 11 : 40 in the morning ____________

b. 5 : 20 in the evening ____________

c. 2 : 30 after midnight ____________

d. 10 : 45 at night ____________

e. One hour before midnight ____________

f. 3 o' clock in the afternoon ____________

g. Three hours after 11 a. m. ____________

h. Three hours before 3.20 p. m. ____________

i. 30 minutes after 11.30 p. m. ____________

j. 50 minutes after 12 noon ____________

k. 30 minutes before 4.30 a. m. ____________

l. 2 hours after 12 noon ____________

The 24-hour clock

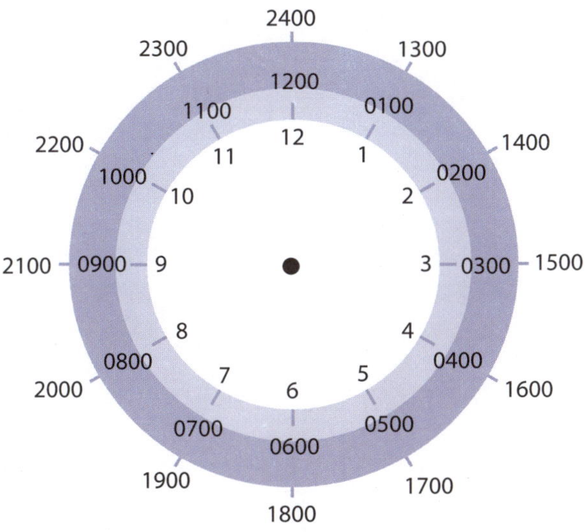

Railways, air services, defence forces, television network, shipping lines throughout the world use the 24 hour clock.

They do not use a. m. or p. m. In this

12 midnight	**is**	**0000 Hours**	
1 a. m	is	0100 hours	
3.30 a. m	is	0330 hours	
10.45 a. m	is	1045 hours	
12 noon	is	1200 hours	
1 p. m	is	1300 hours	(12 +1 hours)
4.15 p. m	is	1615 hours	(12+4.15=1615)
10 p. m	is	2200 hours	
11.45 pm	is	2345 hours	
12 midnight	**is**	**also written as 2400 hours**	

[the first 2 digits show the hours, next 2 digits show the minutes]

Exercise 12.3

1. Change into 24 hour clock time.

a. 4. 30 p. m	f. 9. 50 a. m
b. 11. 45 p. m	g. 12 midnight
c. 6.15 p. m	h. 4.10 p. m
d. 10. 53 a. m	I. 7. 55 a. m
e. 8. 45 p. m	j. 5.35 p. m

2. Change into 12 hour clock time.

a. 0030 hours	e. 1700 hours
b. 2205 hours	f. 1315 hours
c. 0940 hours	g. 0100 hours
d. 2110 hours	h. 2050 hours

Addition and subtraction of time

1. Add 4 hours 30 mins to 2 hours 45 minutes

hours	min
[1] 4	30
+2	45
6	75
7	15

30 min + 45 min = 75 mins

= 60 + 15

= 1 hr 15 mins

Answer: 15 minutes

2. Find the difference between 3 hours 20 mins and 2 hours 30 minutes.

hours	min
[1] 3	[80] 20
−2	30
	50

2 < 3

so, borrow 1 hour = 60 mins from 3 hours

so, in mins column you have 60 + 20 = 80 mins and 3 – 1 = 2 hours column.

Answer: 50 minutes

Time duration

EXAMPLE

Lunch break in a school is from 10.10 a. m. to 10.40 a. m. Find the duration of the break.

Sol: Time duration of the break is the time interval between 10.10 a. m. and 10.40 a. m.

This can be found by subtraction

	hours	min
10.40 a. m can be written as	10	40
10.10 a. m. can be written as	10	10
	0	30

Answer: 30 minutes

EXAMPLE

A school starts at 7.30 a. m. and ends at 2 p. m. Find the time duration.

Sol: Here the school starts at 7.30 a. m. and ends at 2 p. m. the time interval can he found by 2 methods.

I method

1.Convert to 24 hr clock.

hours	min
~~14~~ (3)	~~00~~ (60)
−7	30
6	30

7.30 a. m is 0730 hrs

2 p. m. is 1400 hrs.

Answer: 6 hours 30 mins

II method

2.This is by counting ahead till 12 noon. It is 4 h 30 min and then adding 2 h (12 to 2 p. m.) total is 6 h 30 mins.

Exercise 12.4

1. Find the time interval for the following.

a. 5.10 a. m. to 8.50 a.m.

b. 4.15 a. m. to 3.10 p. m.

c. 11.55 p. m to 11.45 a. m.

d. 3.20 a. m. to 11. 10 a.m.

e. 9.20 a. m. to 11.45 p. m.

f. 12.30 a. m. to 12.30 p. m.

2. Find the time

a. 2 hours before 1.50 p. m. __________

b. 4 hours after 12 midnight __________

c. 3 hours before 12 noon __________

d. 6 hours 15 mins before 7.10 a.m__________

e. 2 hours 40 minutes after 8.30 p. m __________

3.

a. 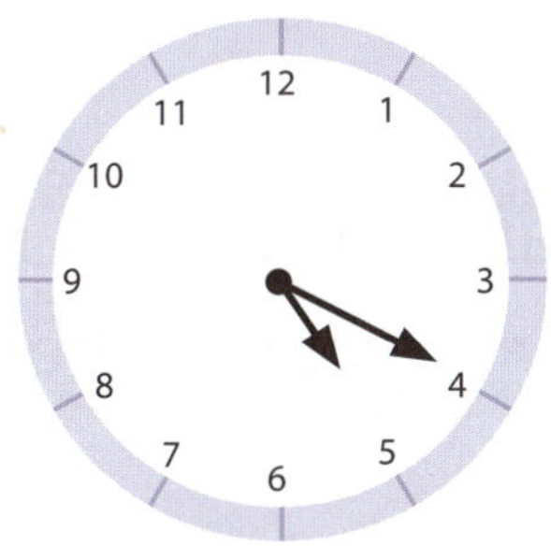

What was the time 15 minutes earlier?

b. 

What time was it 30 minutes earlier?

c. 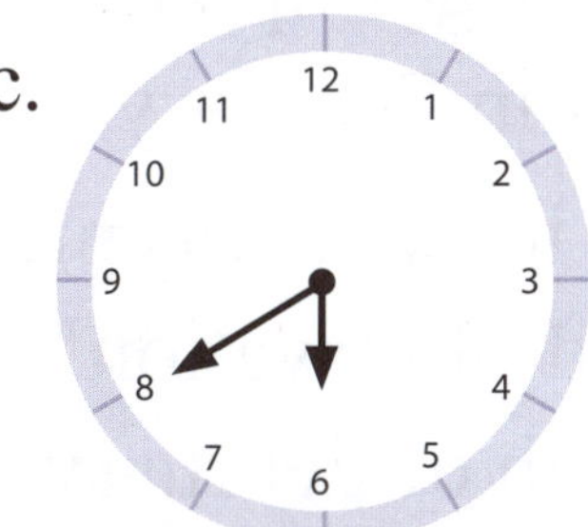

What time was it 50 minutes earlier?

4. Fill in the time

a. Ashok was scheduled to arrive at the airport at 7 pm. His flight was delayed by 2 hours 25 minutes. So he arrived at __________.

b. Rahul went to watch a 11 a. m. show. It was a 100 minutes movie. The show got over at __________.

c. Sheila goes to office at 9.15 a.m. and returns at 7 p. m. She works for __________ hours and __________ minutes.

d. The match started at 11.30 a. m. It was for 1 hour 45 minutes. It got over at __________.

Calendar

The teacher was showing the calendar of the year 2011 and talking about number of days in different months, in a year.

She pointed to the calendar and said, 'January, March, May, July, August, October and December have 31 days.

April, June, September, November have 30 days. February has 28 days. So, a year has 365 days.'

Rahul got up and said. 'Madam, I saw the calendar of 2012, it has 29 days in February.'

The teacher was pleased and patted him on his back and said, 'Yes Rahul good observation! February has 29 days once every 4 years. The year, month of February, has 29 days is called a leap year.'

A year has 365 ¼ days. But we normally take 1 year to have 365 days.

A **leap year** has 366 days and that year February has 29 days.

> A leap year is divisible by 4. So, 2011 is not a leap year but 2012 is. Can you name a few leap years?

Time Interval in Days

EXAMPLE

Rajesh went to Goa on 25 December and returned on 10 January. How long did he stay in Goa?

Answer: Days in December 31–24 = 7 days

Days in January 10

17 days

Note: Many children subtract 25 from 31 which is incorrect. 25th is included, so it should be 31-24.

Exercise 12.5

1. Calculate the number of days
   a. 13 February to 17 March (in a leap year)
   b. 24 November to 14 January
2. Summer holidays were from May 20 to July 4. They were for ____________ days.
3. The autumn break is for 9 days from 7 October to ____________ .
4. On 6 Dec, Rama said "2 weeks more and holidays will begin." On which date did the holidays begin? ____________

Money

13

Recap

Convert into paise

a. ₹ 17.50 ____________ c. ₹ 38.20 ____________

b. ₹ 40.40 ____________ d. ₹ 50.70 ____________

2. Convert into rupees

a. 6375 p ____________ c. 1407 p ____________

b. 9290 p ____________ d. 625 p ____________

3. Put '>' or '<'

a. ₹ 110 ☐ ₹ 100 + ₹ 100

b. ₹ 50 ☐ 5001 p

c. ₹ 30 + ₹ 30 ☐ 6000 p

d. 7999 p ☐ ₹ 4 + ₹ 76

e. 4375 p ☐ ₹ 42

f. 8665 p ☐ 8865

Making a bill

EXAMPLE

Shweta bought a skirt for ₹ 650.00, a book for ₹ 290.50 and a blouse for ₹ 1205.75. How much money did she spend? Make a bill.

Bill	₹	650.00
Skirt	₹	650.00
Book	₹	+ 290.50
Blouse	₹	+ 1205.75
	₹	2146.25

Answer: Shweta spent ₹ 2146.25

Exercise 13.1

1. Make a bill in each case and find the total money.

   a. A wristband for ₹ 137.90, a head band for ₹ 350.00 and a basket ball for ₹ 509.55.

   b. A school bag for ₹ 300.00 pencil box for ₹ 95.60, a tiffin box for ₹ 80.75 and a water bottle for ₹ 106.85.

2. Students collected money. On the first day they collected ₹ 595.25, on the second day ₹ 1200.60. They put some money from their own savings and donated ₹ 2000. How much did they add from their savings?

3. Neha had ₹ 800. She spent ₹ 425.50 on Monday, ₹ 176.85 on Tuesday. How much money is left with her?

Multiplication and division of money

Multiplication of money is the same as multiplication of numbers. The dot '.' between rupees and paise has to be put carefully.

EXAMPLE

Cost of 1 pencil is ₹ 12.10 find the cost of 6 such pencils.

Solution: Cost of 1 pencil = ₹ 12.10

Cost of 6 pencils = × 6

72.60

Answer: Cost of 6 pencils = ₹ 72.60

EXAMPLE

Cost of 1 eraser is ₹ 8. How many can be bought for ₹ 320?

Solution: We divide 320 by 8

```
   H T O
     4 0
   ______
8 ) 3 2 0
  - 3 2
  ------
    x x 0
        0
      ---
        x
      ---
```

Q =40, it is the number of erasers that can be bought for ₹ 320.

Exercise 13.2

1. Find the cost of the following
   a. Cost of 1 pillow is ₹ 210, find cost of 9 such pillows.
   b. 8 books if one book costs ₹ 106.75
2. Find the cost of:
   a. 1 jacket if 5 jackets cost ₹ 3505.
   b. 1 shirt of 6 shirts cost ₹ 4086.
3. Cost of 1 pencil box is ₹ 7. How many pencil boxes can be bought for ₹ 1826? How much money will be left?

4. Sheela had ₹ 500. Her mother gave her ₹ 350 more. With that she bought 4 pairs of socks for ₹ 134.75 per pair. How much money is left with her?

Mental Math

1. What is the cost of
   a. 3 watches if 1 watch costs ₹ 200 ____________
   b. 1 belt if 5 belts cost ₹ 350 ____________
   c. 1 eraser if 10 erasers cost ₹ 26.50 ____________
2. Which is greater ₹ 300.00 or ₹ 246.60 + ₹ 64.40
3. A box has 15 coins in a box. There are equal numbers of ₹ 10, ₹ 2 and Re 1 coins. How much money is there in the box?

Patterns

14

Recap

Complete the patterns

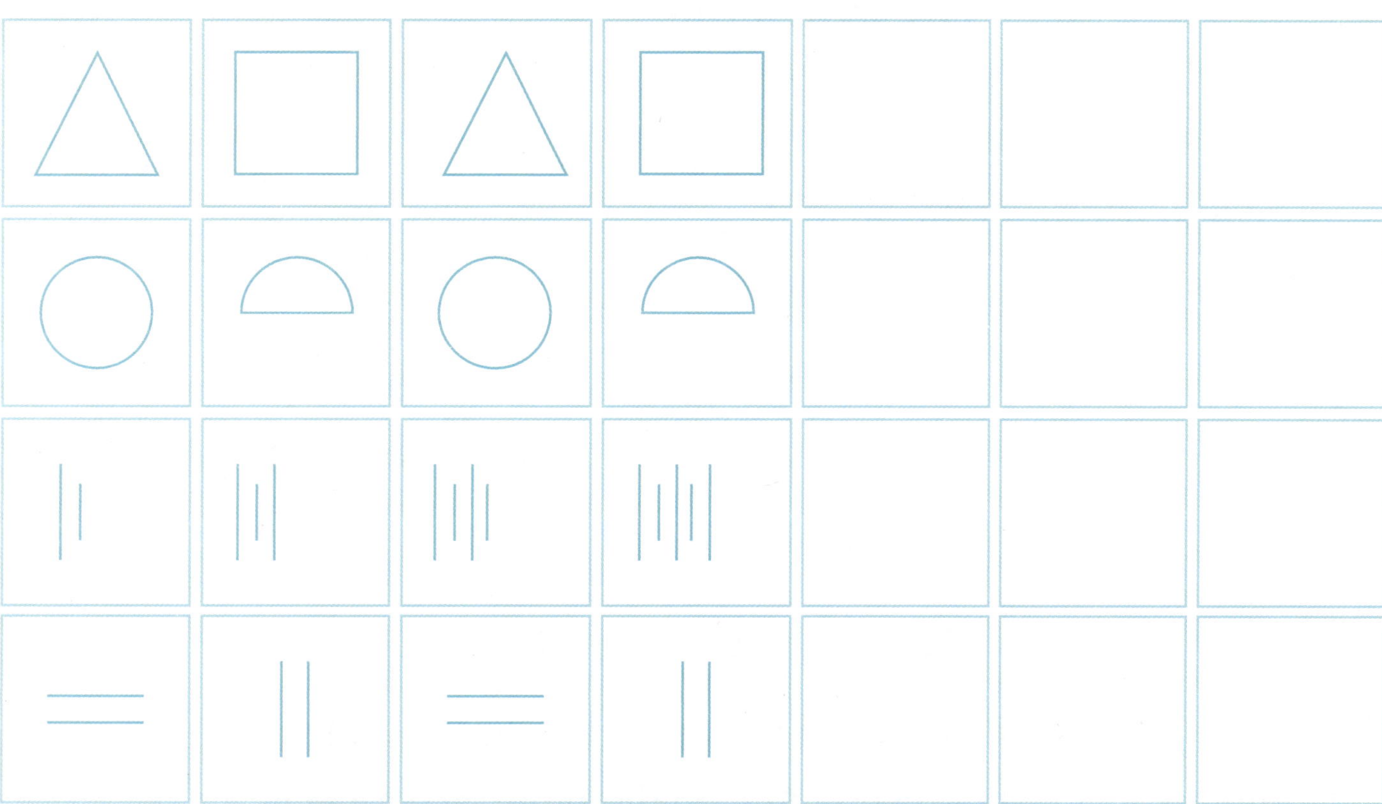

Patterns in numbers

A series of numbers follow a pattern. If we understand the pattern we can find the next numbers of the series.

EXAMPLE

5 9 13 17 21 25 29

$5 + 4 = 9 + 4 = 13 + 4 = 17 + 4 = 21$

Terms increase by 4

EXAMPLE

14 12 10

$14 + 2 = 12 - 2 = 10 - 2 = 8$

Terms decrease by 2

Number towers

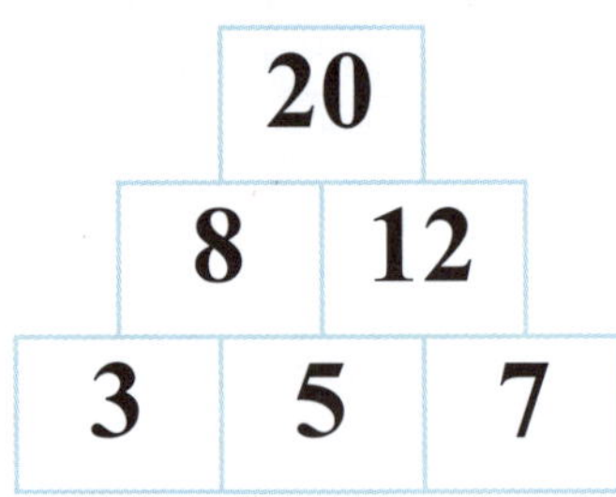

We can make towers using multiplication, subtraction or division.

Add two numbers in boxes and write sum in box above them.

Codes

Important information can be written in a coded language. Secrets or information is sent in this manner.

A number code could be like this

Z	Y	X	W	V	U	T	S	R	Q	P	O
1	2	3	4	5	6	7	8	9	10	11	12

A	B	C	D	E	F	G	H	I	J	K	L	M	N
26	25	24	23	22	21	20	19	18	17	16	15	14	13

To read such message we need to have a key to the code.
Decoding is a very interesting and challenging experience.

EXAMPLE

BE QUIET → 25 22 10 6 18 22 7

GREAT → 20 9 22 26 7

A lot many more codes can be generated.

Exercise 14.1

1. Complete the pattern given below

   a. 3, 23, 43, _______, _______, _______, _______

   b. 194, 192, 190, _______, _______, _______, _______

c. A2, B1, C2, ______, ______, ______, ______

d. ZY, XW, VU, ______, ______, ______, ______

e. 2020, 2010, 2000, ______, ______, ______, ______

2. Fill the blanks and make the following number pyramids.

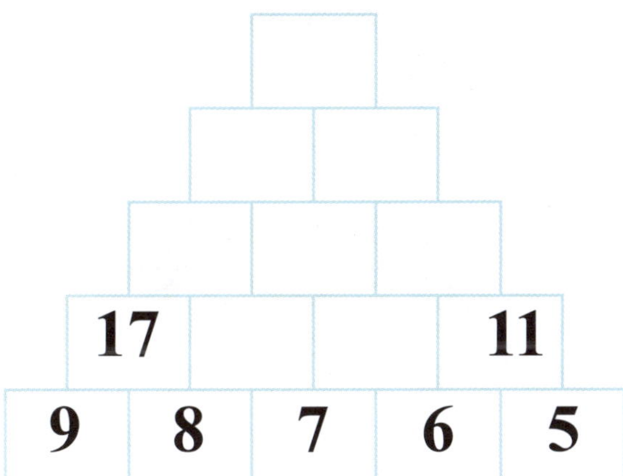

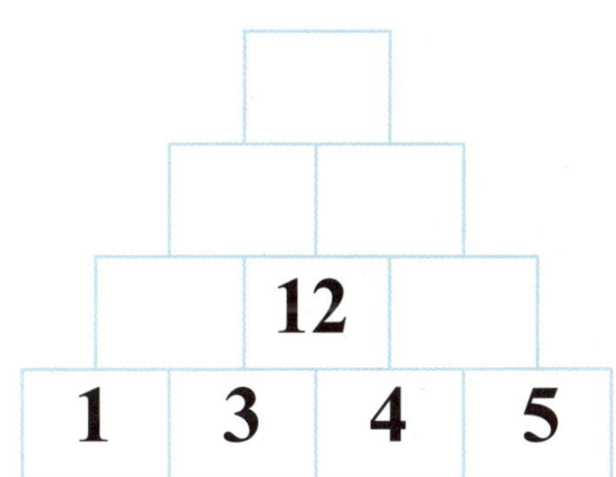

3. Decode the message

a. 9 113 91449114

b. 711489109 – 9 191325 – 85 18 15

c. 9 12 15225 3189 3 11 520

4. Write in codes

a. BE PATIENT

b. BE HONEST

c. NEVER LIE

Data-Handling

15

Children of a group were asked about their favourite fast food. This is how their preference was recorded. (Remember: Eating too much fast food injures our health)

Let us make the tally chart for this information.

Food	Tally Marks	No. of children
Pizza	~~1111~~ 1	6
Burger	~~1111~~ 11	7
Chicken sandwich	111	3
Hot dog	111	3
Noodles	1	1

This information can be shown with the help of a pictograph.

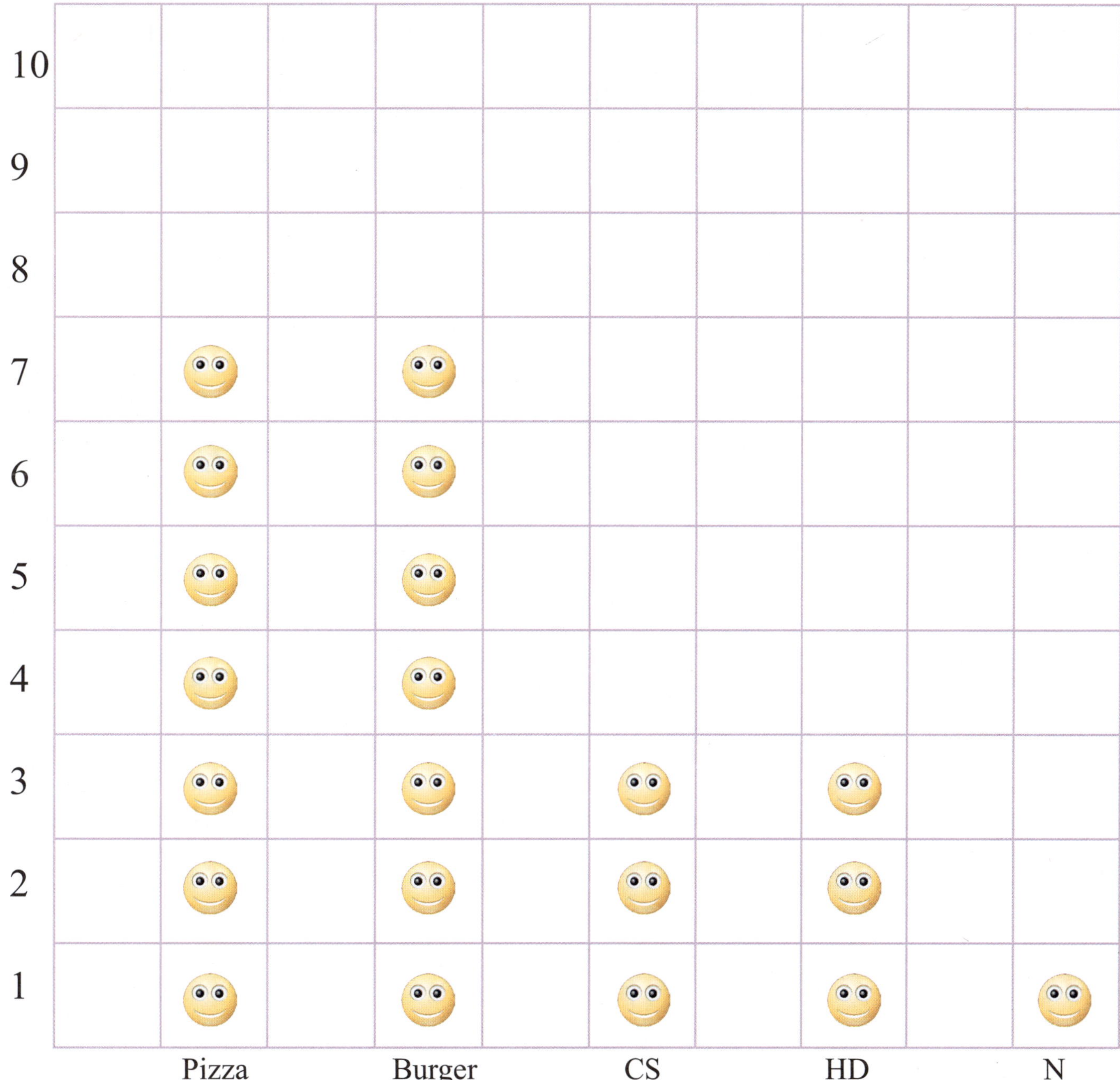

Favourite Fast Food

Answer the following

1. Which is the most popular fast food?
2. Which is least popular?
3. What fraction of children liked Burger?
4. How many more children like Pizza than Hot dog?

Bar Graphs

This is a graph where instead of pictures rectangles called bars are drawn.

The following graph shows the number of comics the children have

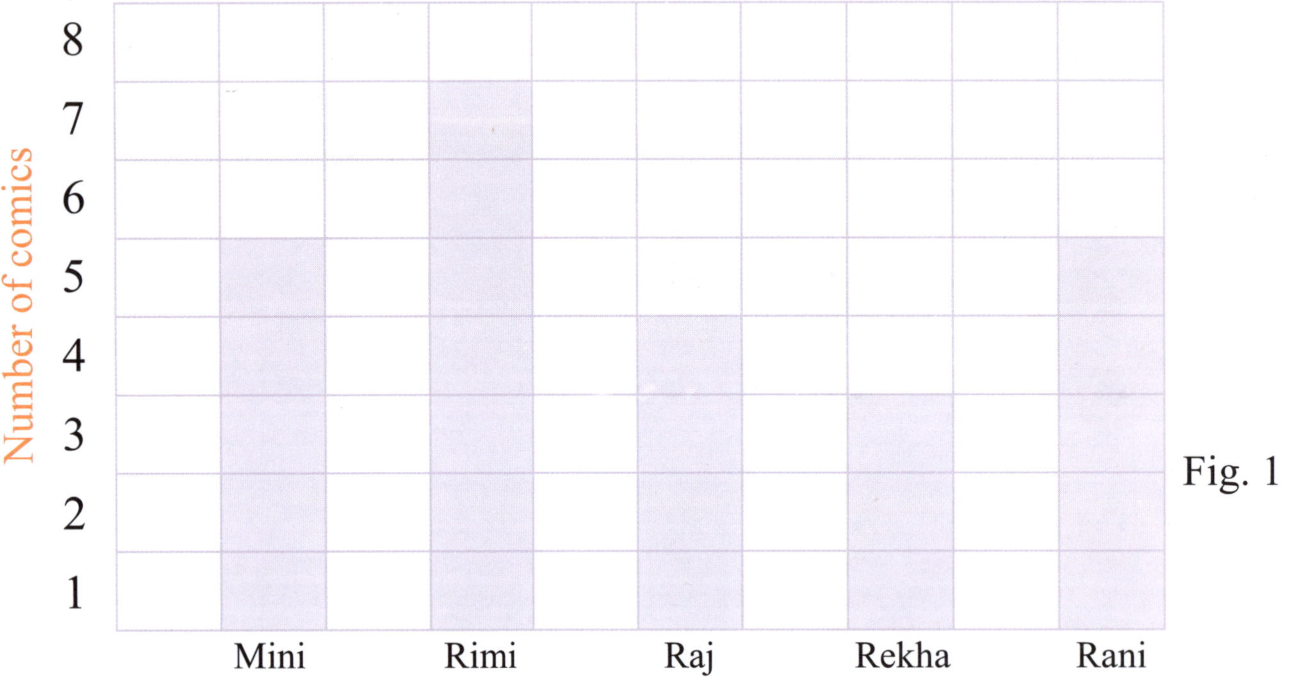

Fig. 1

Exercise 15.1

This is a bar graph showing the favourite sport of some students (by voting).

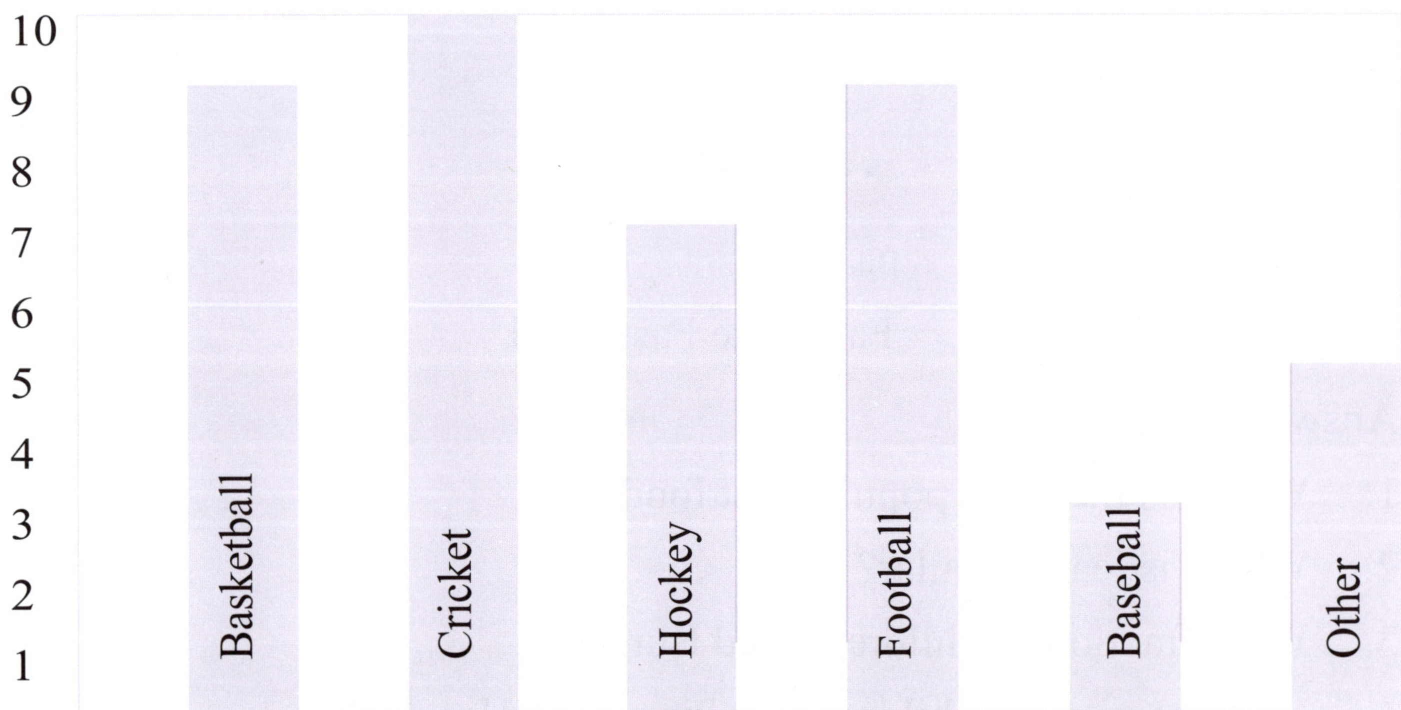

Fig. 2

1. Answer the following (Refer to fig 2 on pg 134)
   a. Which sport is most popular?
   b. How many more students voted for Cricket than Hockey?
   c. How many students voted for the least popular sport?
   d. How many students voted in all?
2. Read the given information carefully and prepare the required bar graph.

   Scores of 6 players

Player	Salil	Robert	Akash	Dhruv	Abeer	Vikram
Points	200	250	350	300	150	250

{Hint Take 1 box = 50 points}

3. Answer the following questions (refer to fig. 1)
   a. Who has the highest number of comics?
   b. Name two children who have the same number of comics?
   c. How many comics does Raj have?
   d. Who has the least number of comics?
4. Choices of favourite fruits by a group of people. Read the graph and answer the questions.

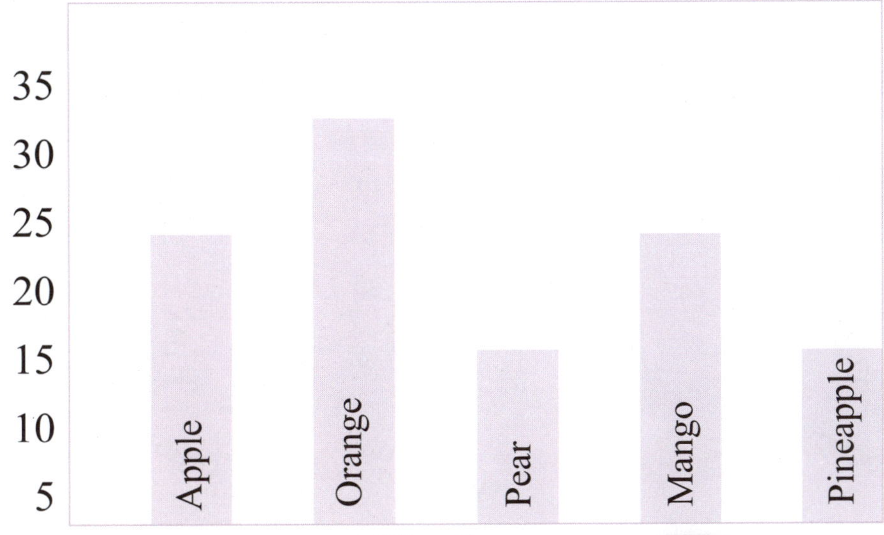

Fig. 3

   a. How many people chose apple?
   b. Which fruit is most popular?
   c. Which two fruits are equally liked?
   d. Which fruit is the least popular?

Data Handling

Objective: To learn to collect information and represent data

Materials required: Graph paper, colours, pencil

Method: Students are divided into group of 4.

Each group is asked to choose a topic on which they will collect information.

Example

Favourite sport (out of 5)

Favourite fruit (out of 5)

Cricketer (out of 5)

1. Favourite player (out of 5)
2. Favourite Harry Potter movie (out of 5)
3. Two students collect information and two record it
4. Then they use tally marks to tabulate the information.
5. This information is to be represented on a graph paper (or square lined paper) using appropriate scale depending on the strength of the class.
6. Every bar graph should have an appropriate title

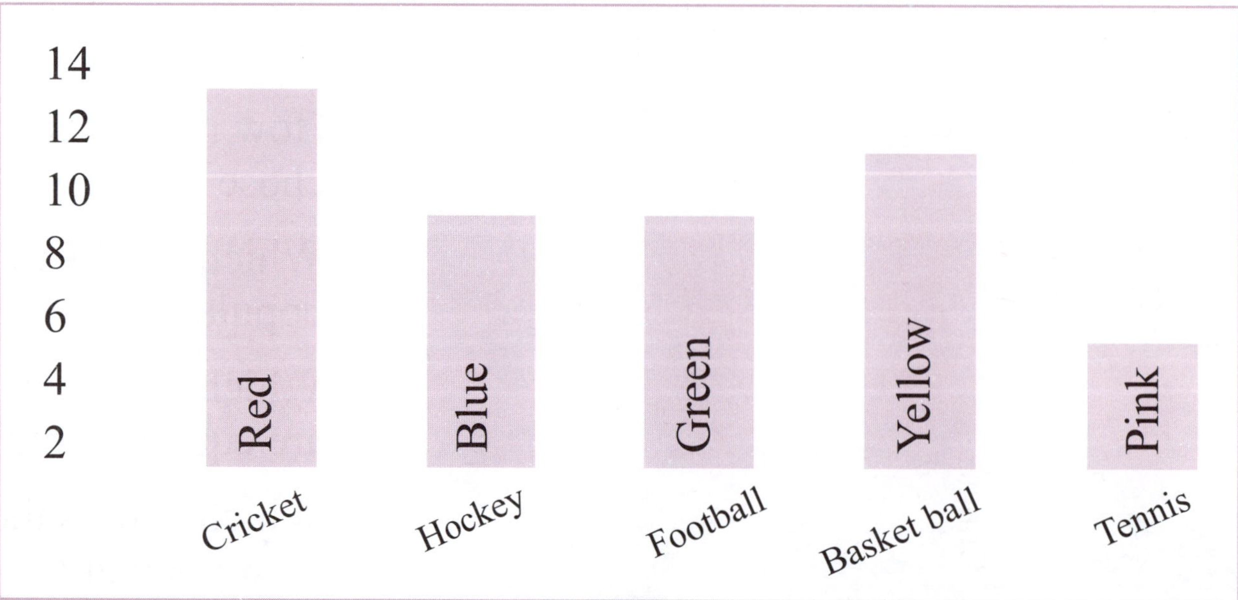

REVIEW EXERCISE 1

1. Fill in the blanks

   a. Smallest 6-digit number is ________.

   b. 1 lakh = ________ thousands = ________ ten thousands

   c. 3 thousand more than 97,000 is ________.

   d. Predecessor of 87,000 is ________.

   e. Raju was born in 2007. His father is 30 years older than Raju. His father was born in ________.

   f. 16000 is ________ more than 15500.

   g. 400000 + 60000 + 1 + 8000 = ________.

   h. 530040 = 5 × ________ + ________ × 10000 + ________ × 100 + ________ × 100 + – × 10 + 0 × ________.

   i. Place value of 7 in 178015 according to Indian System of Numeration is ________.

   j. 3287 rounded to the nearest 100 is ________.

2. Write number names for the following in Indian as well as International System of Numeration.

   a. 650003 ______________________________

   b. 390500 ______________________________

3. Write the numerals for

   a. Four lakhs and ten ____________

   b. five hundred and thirty thousand ____________

4. Subtract 325439 from 400001

5. There were 6, 50, 147 bags of wheat in a godown. On Monday 2,38,280 were taken out and on Tuesday 3,07,169 were taken out. How many bags were left in the godown on Wednesday?

6. Write the predecessor of

   a. xix ______________________

   b. xxxi ______________________

   c. Xl ______________________

   d. 1 ______________________

8. Successor of a number is 1 lakh. What is the number?

9. Raj and Manju collect stamps. Together they have 345 stamps. If Manju has 208 stamps, find the number of stamps Raj has.

10. Find the number which exceeds

    68534 by 5729

11. Fill in the blanks

    a. Seven thousand less than 36,421 is __________

    b. 1 more than 10000 is __________

    c. 3 hundred more than 68,720 is __________

    d. 4 thousand more than 88888 is __________

    e. The successor of the greatest 5-digit numeral is __________

REVIEW EXERCISE 2

1. 1000 added 6 times is equal to __________. 150 added 8 times is equal to __________

   a. 150 added 8 times is equal to __________

   b. 3 times 1700 is equal to __________

2. Difference in the place value of 2 eights in 8182 is __________

   a. 6890 is __________ more than 6570

   b. 7818 is __________ less than 7900

4. Write and add only the successors

   a. 2359 __________

   b. 1839 __________

   c. 3076 __________

5. On Friday 1280 persons visited a mall. On Saturday 250 more people visited. On Sunday, the number of people who visited the mall were 750 more than that on Saturday. How many persons visited on Sunday?

6. 3450 is subtracted from a number gives 4464. What is the number?

7. Add 11 hours 29 minutes, 5 hours 23 minutes, 7 hours 23 minutes and 25 minutes.

8. Sonia studies for 2 hour 15 minutes in the morning. In the afternoon she studies 45 minutes less than that in the morning but at night

she studies 1 hour 30 minutes more than that in the afternoon. How much time does she study altogether?

9. Mrs. Sharma starts her journey at 11 am from city A to go to city B. She stops on the way for 50 minutes for snacks. After sometime she stops again for 15 minutes to buy wire. This whole journey took 4 hr 40 minutes. What time would she have reached city B if she, had not stopped any where else?

10. A carton can carry 135 kg. There are 20 boxes each one weighing 9 kg. How many of these boxes can the carton carry?

REVIEW EXERCISE 3

1. Find the product of

a. $\begin{array}{r} 248 \\ \times 12 \\ \hline \\ \hline \end{array}$ b. $\begin{array}{r} 367 \\ \times 24 \\ \hline \\ \hline \end{array}$ c. $\begin{array}{r} 439 \\ \times 48 \\ \hline \\ \hline \end{array}$ d. $\begin{array}{r} 767 \\ \times 123 \\ \hline \\ \hline \end{array}$ e. $\begin{array}{r} 880 \\ \times 374 \\ \hline \\ \hline \end{array}$

f. $\begin{array}{r} 4540 \\ \times 36 \\ \hline \\ \hline \end{array}$ g. $\begin{array}{r} 328 \\ \times 19 \\ \hline \\ \hline \end{array}$ h. $\begin{array}{r} 3818 \\ \times 22 \\ \hline \\ \hline \end{array}$ i. $\begin{array}{r} 2408 \\ \times 79 \\ \hline \\ \hline \end{array}$

2. Make the smallest and the largest numbers using the digits 5, 0, 9, 6 (using digits only once)

3. Cost of a Lazy Boy chair is ₹ 9750. Find the cost of 35 such chairs?

4. A truck can carry 1450 kg. There are 180 boxes each weighing 9 kg. How many of these boxes can the truck carry?

5. 3450 subtracted from a number gives 4485. What is the number?

6. Anil's father is 34 Years old. His grandfather is 30 years older than Anil's father. His grandmother is 26 years older than Anil's father. How old are Anil's grandfather and grandmother?

7. 528 pencils were bundled together into 9 equal bundles. How many pencils were there in each bundle and how many were left out?

8. Mr. Kumar left home for work at 8.45 a. m. His wife left 30 minutes later. She left home at ________.

REVIEW EXERCISE 4

1. Write the number which is 3000 more than 18,909.
2. Write the difference of the smallest 5-digit number and the greatest 3-digit number.
3. What number exceeds 2,38,947 by 3623?
4. Find the difference in the population of the two cities if population of city A is 1,37,640 and that of city B is 2,01,082.
5. The sum of two numbers is 86,729. If one number is 38,940 find the other number.
6. The same number is missing in both places. Choose the correct number and fill the blank spaces.

$$\begin{array}{r} 7\ 8\ 6\ 5 \\ -\ 6\ \square\ 2\ 9 \\ \hline 1\ \square\ 3\ 6 \\ \hline \end{array}$$

a. 4 b. 5 c. 6 d. 7

7. Find the sum of 27435; 32468 and 2109.
8. Mr. Mehra had ₹ 36,468 in his bank account. He withdraws ₹ 9,790. How much money is left in his account?
9. Round each number to nearest thousand

a. 14376 b. 28199 c. 72949 d. 5038

REVIEW EXERCISE 5

1. Find the quotient and remainder

a.	9246 ÷ 17	b.	9400 ÷ 92
c.	8640 ÷ 50	d.	7938 ÷ 17
e.	3824 ÷ 24	f.	6945 ÷ 38
g.	8299 ÷ 21	h.	2768 ÷ 18
i.	1824 ÷ 22	j.	6716 ÷ 14

2. Product of 2 numbers is 3328. If one number is 52 find the other number.

3. Rama has ₹ 7050 in her purse. She has only ₹ 50 notes. How many notes does she have?

4. One crate of eggs can hold 24 eggs. A poultry farm owner has 5520 eggs. How many crates will be required for 5520 eggs?

5. 9630 crayons can be packed in 15 cartons. How many crayons will be there in each carton?

6. Find the common factors of

   60, 24, 81

7. Write equivalent fractions of

   a. 3/7 : ________ ________ ________

   b. 1/4 : ________ ________ ________

   c. 2/5 : ________ ________ ________

REVIEW EXERCISE 6

1. Add

   a. 26 km 475 m and 18 km 950 m

   b. 4 kg 250 g, 8 kg 650 g and 27 kg 30 g

   c. 24 l 555 ml, 36 l 46 ml and 9 l 5 ml

2. Subtract

   a. 35l 750 ml from 48 l 225 ml

   b. 29 kg 400g from 31 kg 750 g

3. A container of paint has 25 l of red paint 18 l 250 ml was used in painting a wall. How much paint was left in the container?

4. To decorate the school for the Annual Day 1400 bulbs were bought. If the cost of each bulb is ₹ 25, find the total cost of 1400 bulbs.

5. 5 friends together purchased a cricket kit for ₹ 7925. Find the money given by each friend.

6. If there are 1705 students and 8525 sweets. How many sweets will each child get?

7. 123 bags of rice can be loaded in a ship. How many ships are needed to load 31611 such bags?

Answers

CHAPTER 1

1. a. Four thousand three hundred forty
   b. Seven thousand nineteen
   c. Eight thousand five hundred ninety eight
   d. Six thousand nine hundred fourteen
   e. Three thousand seven hundred eleven
   f. Five thousand sixty three
   g. Two thousand four hundred seventeen
   h. One thousand eight hundred five

2. a. 3004 b. 5077 c. 5080 d. 6044
   e. 8008 f. 4000 g. 1234

3. a. 8046 b. 6003 c. 4705 d. 2938

4. a. 4000 + 300 + 40 + 0 b. 7000 + 500 + 0 + 1
   c. 3000 + 0 + 40 + 0 d. 1000 + 800 + 0 + 6
   e. 8000 + 700 + 40 + 9 f. 6000 + 0 + 0 + 5

5. a. 5468, 5486, 5684, 5864 b. 420, 3120, 5030, 6010
   c. 7136, 7306, 7603, 7630 d. 89, 98, 192, 312

6. a. 3881, 3801, 3108, 3081 b. 8888, 6666, 5555, 4444
   c. 7605, 7504, 7465, 754 d. 6423, 4236, 3426, 2436

7. a. 999 b. 9998

8. a. 933 b. 981 c. 8625 d. 8369

e. 8800 f. 7110 g. 7214

9. a. 527 b. 1258 c. 1686 d. 990
   e. 166 f. 506 g. 1289 h. 1121

10. a. 1352 b. 1512 c. 3478 d. 16665
    e. 12980 f. 7259 g. 12900 h. 3663

11. a. 120 b. 71 c. 34 d. 112
    e. 62, R 1 f. 120, R 4 g. 181, R 0 h. 188, R 0

12. a. 2450 b. 3000 c. 70.35 d. 12000
    e. 5 f. 7200 g. 240 h. 5
    i. 6 j. 4

14. a. 8:20, 20 minutes past 8 b. 2:15, Quarter past 2

CHAPTER 2

Exercises 2.1

2. a. 3,00,026 b. 2,00,700 c. 5,00,030 d. 8,08,400 e. 94,090

3. a. 69,200; 70,200; 71,200; b. 3,02,504; 3,02,604; 3,02,704
   c. 6,56,789; 7,56789; 8,56,789;

Exercises 2.2

1. a. 6000 b. 6 c. 800 d. 30,000
   e. 9,00,000 f. 1000 g. 0 h. 1

2. a. 8, 6, 5, 3, 4

b. 3, 10,000, 6, 100, 10, 1

c. 20,000, 9000, 500, 40, 0

3. a. 30,000 + 7,000 + 0 + 10 + 8

   b. 40,00,000 + 2,00,000 + 90,000 + 7,000 + 800 + 10 + 6

   c. 8,00,000 + 6,000 + 1

   d. 20,00,000 + 40

   e. 4,00,000 + 6,000 + 30 + 8

   f. 5,00,000 + 50,000 + 400 + 3

4. a. 7,08,707 b. 8,080 c. 30,033

   d. 5,627 e. 7,26,480

Exercises 2.3

1. a. $<$ b. $>$ c. $>$ d. $>$ e. $>$ f. $>$ g. $>$ h. $>$

2. a. 19670, 20648, 54187, 65771

   b. 209568, 278934, 396452, 814792

   c. 168390, 268750, 278934, 284570

3. a. 598175, 584725, 569875, 548275

   b. 25962, 25629, 25296, 25269

   c. 282669, 228966, 228696, 28962

Exercises 2.4

1. a. 865210, 102568 b. 98760, 60879

   c. 986510, 105689 d. 654210, 102456

   e. 874210, 102478

2. a. 570198 b. 100009 c. 439099 d. 679899 e. 934099

3. a. 610001 b. 900910 c. 301007 d. 273460 e. 27404

4. 100000; One lakh

5. 99999; ninety nine thousand nine hundred ninety nine

Exercises 2.5

1. a. 1,85,602; 185,602 b. 3,00,246; 300,246
   c. 42,81,510; 4,281,510 d. 50,00,000; 5,000,000
   e. 2,15,746; 215,746

4. a. 3,01,020 b. 47,47,407 c. 304,306 d. 5,206,080
   e. 90,090

Exercises 2.6

1. a. 70 b. 36970 c. 180 d. 70990
   e. 2480 f. 2000

2. a. 26500 b. 78700 c. 384300 d. 477900
   e. 849600 f. 5,55,600

Exercises 2.7

1. a. 36500 b. 154000 c. 47000 d. 11000 e. 56000

Exercises 2.8

1. a.

19	26	29	34	39	40	44	49	54	59	1	71	84	89
XIX	XXVI	XXIX	XXXIV	XXXIX	XL	XLIV	XLIX	LIV	LIX	I	LXXI	LXXXIV	LXXXIX

   b.

61	83	66	65	46	73	29	38
LXI	LXXXIII	LXVI	LXV	XLVI	LXXIII	XXIX	XXXVIII

2. a. $800000 + 8000 + 100 + 60 + 9 = 808169$

b. 100000 + 9000 + 200 + 70 = 109270

3. No; 6,05,405

Mental Maths

1. 99998　2. 10002　3. 11111　4. 99999　5. 49,500
6. 100

CHAPTER 3

Exercises 3.1

1. a. 400　b. 98001　c. 342102　d. 428

2. a. 1112619　b. 634180　c. 819201　d. 60458
   e. 679330　f. 296838　g. 211691　h. 699706
   i. 275496

3. a. 7400　b. 9380　c. 77000　d. 3500　e. 57500

4. a. 6, 5, 2, 5, 5　b. 4, 1, 7, 6, 3　c. 3, 7, 6, 5, 7
   d. 1, 4, 0, 5, 7　e. 4, 1, 7, 6, 3　f. 2, 7, 3, 4, 3

5. a. 18, 409; 76, 505　b. 65510
   c. 71370　d. 88138
   e. 0　f. 500

Exercises 3.2

1. 65478　2. 2,16,041

3. 3, 90, 995
4. 2, 22, 037
5. 8367
6. 55523
7. 71876

Exercises 3.3

1. ₹ 3400
2. 400 km, 430 km
3. b. 6000 + 1000, 7000
   c. 10000 + 30000, 40000
   d. 50000 + 45000, 95000
   e. 73000 + 30000, 103000

Mental Maths

1. a. 4, 5, 1, 7, 5 b. 8, 8, 0, 5, 5
2. 30
3. 60, 100
4. 1000
5. 500
6. 11, 9
7. 2020

CHAPTER 4

Exercises 4.1

1. a. 10853 b. 13918 c. 6518 d. 636918
   e. 517 f. 82574 g. 35058 h. 16757
   i. 310643

2. a. 34821 b. 59677 c. 7644 d. 34, 628
   e. 4, 23, 210

3. a. 8, 2, 0, 8, 6 b. 1, 0, 0, 6, 5 c. 9, 1, 2, 0, 5 d. 9, 6, 2, 3, 1
   e. 6, 3, 2, 7, 8 f. 4, 8, 2, 4, 8

Exercises 4.2

1. 1071615 2. 44082 3. 5396 4. 118645
5. 30, 000 6. 15, 90, 000

Exercises 4.3

1. a. 40 b. 700
2. a. 400 b. 1000
3. a. 15000 b. 4000
4. 27000

Mental Maths

1. a. 3, 1, 1, 5, 6 b. 9, 4, 1, 5, 4
2. 0
3. 90,000

CHAPTER 5

Exercises 5.1

1. a. 10 b. 0 c. 0 d. 237 e. 46, 78 f. 30
   g. 0 h. 12 i. 72 j. product

Exercises 5.2

1. a. 7000 b. 57000 c. 19200 d. 90000 e. 50000 f. 16000
   g. 660000 h. 27600 i. 9600 j. 120000

2. a. 1220000 b. 274000 c. 9600 d. 35100 e. 75000 f. 5200
g. 642000 h. 255500 i. 8000 j. 21600

Exercises 5.3

1. a. 7, 50, 200, 257; 166536
   b. 139, 139, 200, 246; 34194

2. a. 45151 b. 58650 c. 171010 d. 228726 e. 274340
   f. 105046 g. 223716 h. 97960 i. 123136 j. 168630
   k. 222250 l. 411037 m. 31496 n. 279748 o. 63000

Exercises 5.4

1. a. ₹ 1785000 b. 119102 c. 94400 d. 72072
   e. 615000 f. 34320 g. 9989001 h. 744

Exercises 5.5

1. a. 700 b. 2350 c. 2050 d. 460 e. 760
   f. 4050 g. 2240 h. 2460

2. a. 100100 b. 157700 c. 462400 d. 130700 e. 284900
   f. 37400 g. 64000 h. 112900

Mental Maths

1. a. 20000 b. 90000 c. 6 d. 1000
   e. 1000 f. 35

2. 4734000 3. 843000 4. 90 5. 700

CHAPTER 6

Exercises 6.1

1. a. 0 b. 0 c. 234 d. 1 e. 45, 9, 5
   f. $56 \div 7 = 8$ g. 10 h. 7 i. 9 j. 9
   k. 7 l. 9 m. 8 n. 8 o. 9

Exercises 6.2

a. 6 b. 480 c. 278 d. 8 e. 73
f. 763 g. 30 h. 904 i. 36 j. 520
k. 14 l. 51

Exercises 6.3

a. 25; 1 b. 20; 3 c. 140; 4 d. 753; 6 e. 49; 0
f. 78; 5 g. 833; 1 h. 1633; 4 i. 13; 3 j. 55; 0
k. 823; 1 l. 140; 2 m. 144; 0 n. 56; 3 o. 523; 5
p. 1077; 7

Exercises 6.4

1. a. 5; 10 b. 20; 0 c. 266; 10 d. 94; 29 e. 2; 14
   f. 11; 25 g. 172; 8 h. 20; 4 i. 25; 6 j. 8; 21
   k. 289; 0 l. 642; 8 m. 11; 7 n. 13; 41 o. 77; 34
   p. 125; 21

2. a. 1893 b. (18,) c. 2 d. 26

Exercises 6.5

1. a. 54; 60　b. 68; 6　c. 12; 634　d. 390; 5　e. 4; 70
   f. 7　g. 90　h. 90; 86　i. 25; 600　j. 4; 280
   k. 3; 40　l. 6; 875

Exercises 6.6

1. 37　2. 5; 14　3. 24　4. 136; 6　5. 25
6. 109　7. 25; 24　8. 680　9. 693

Exercises 6.7

1. a. 4　b. 3　c. 10　d. 16　e. 35

Patterns in Division

1. d. 2000　e. 20,000　f. 2,00,000

3. d. 4　e. 5　f. 6

5. d. 1234　e. 12345, 6

Mental Maths

1. 78345　2. 26943　3. 10　4. 450700
5. One, 500　6. 901　7. 48, 6

CHAPTER 7

Exercises 7.1

1. a. 30, 40, 50, 60　b. 12, 16, 20, 24
   c. 16, 24, 32, 40　d. 22, 33, 44, 55

e. 14, 21, 28, 35

2. a. 3 b. 9, 9, 4 c. 9, 72, 9 d. 7, 49, 7 e. 1, 1

3. 6, 14

4. 9, 5, 15, 61, 55

5. a. Yes b. No c. No d. Yes e. Yes

Exercises 7.2

1. a. 1, 5,25 b. 1, 2, 4, 5, 10, 20
   c. 1, 23 d. 1, 2, 3, 4, 6, 9, 12, 36
   e. 1, 3, 5, 9, 15, 45 f. 1, 17
   g. 1, 2, 3, 6, 9, 18 h. 1, 2, 5, 10, 25, 50
   i. 1, 11 j. 1, 5

2. a. No b. Yes c. No d. No

3. a. 1, 2, 5 b. 1 c. number d. 0
   e. 5, 20, 30, 35 f. limited

4. a. 1, 2, 4, 8, 12 b. 14912
   c. 1, 41 d. 1, 5, 10, 25, 50

Exercises 7.3

1. a. 1 b. 2 c. 1 d. Composite
   e. 1 f. 1, 59

2. a. 2, 3, 5, 7, 11, 13

   b. 23, 29, 31, 37

3. a. 4, 8, 9, 10, 12, 14, 15, 16, 18

   b. 32, 33, 34, 35, 36, 38, 39, 40, 42, 44, 45, 46, 48, 39

4. 17 & 71; 37, 73

Exercises 7.4

1, 2, 3, 4, 6, 8, 12, 24, 1, 2, 4, 8   1, 2, 4, 8, 16, 32

1, 2, 3, 6, 9, 18, 1   1, 5, 7, 35

1, 2, 3, 6, 7, 14, 21, 42, 1, 2, 3, 6   1, 2, 3, 4, 5, 6, 10, 12, 15, 20, 30, 60

Exercises 7.5

1. 2, 4, 88, 324

2. 96

3. c. ✓

4. 36, 102, 72, 98, 900, 3060

5.

Number	Divisible by				
	2	3	5	6	10
518	✓	✗	✗	✗	✗
4320	✓	✓	✓	✓	✓
1000	✓	✗	✓	✗	✓
600	✓	✓	✓	✓	✓
90	✓	✓	✓	✓	✓
80	✓	✗	✓	✗	✓
10	✓	✗	✓	✗	✓

6. a. 20, 25, 30, 35   b. 23, 29   c. 20, 30, 40, 50, 60

7. a. 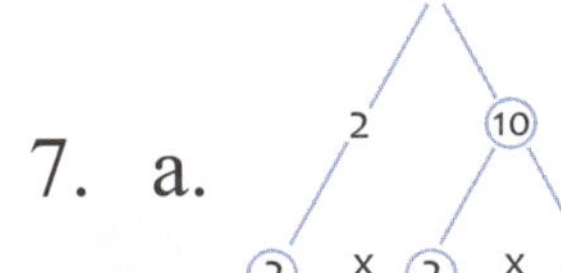

b. 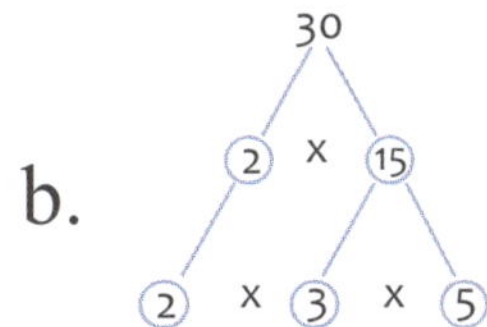

CHAPTER 8

Exercises 8.1

1. $\frac{2}{5}, \frac{8}{15}, \frac{2}{6}, \frac{4}{8}$

2. 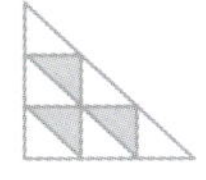 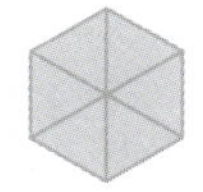 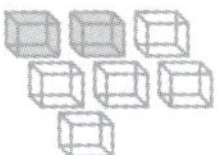

3. a. $\frac{2}{12}$ b. $\frac{1}{4}$

4. a. 7
   b. 4, 11, Four-eleventh
   c. 7, 13
   d. 6, 23, Six-twenty thirdth
   e. 8, 100, Eight hundredth

Exercises 8.2

1. a. 2   b. $\frac{4}{16}$

2. a. $\frac{4}{16}, \frac{8}{12}$ b. $\frac{2}{12}, \frac{3}{18}, \frac{5}{30}$ c. $\frac{30}{40}, \frac{9}{12}$

3. a. 3   b. 2   c. 1   d. 20   e. 50   f. 9

g. 1 h. 40 i. 2 j. 1 k. 1 l. 20

m. 4 n. 13 o. 25 p. 25

Mental Maths

1. a. (ii) 2/7 b. (ii) 2/8

2. a. 25 b. 8 c. 57 d. 1

e. 100 f. 5

3. a. $\frac{7}{14}, \frac{1}{2}$ b. $\frac{100}{200}, \frac{4}{8}, \frac{3}{6}$ c. $\frac{2}{6}, \frac{4}{12}, \frac{6}{18}$

CHAPTER 9

Exercises 9.1

3. a. AB, BC, AC, B, C, A

b. PQ, QR, RS, SP, Q, R, S, P

c. WA, AL, LK, KW, A, L, K, W

Exercises 9.2

1. a. 24 cm b. 18 cm c. 20 cm

2. a. 20 cm b. 32 cm c. 8 cm d. 40 cm

3. b.

4. a. 8 cm b. 13 cm c. 7 cm

5. a. 14 cm b. 14 cm c. 14 cm d. 18 cm

Exercises 9.3

1. a. 9 b. 4 c. 14 d. 12

2. 1. 13 sq cm 2. 13 sq cm 3. 10 sq cm 4. 14 sq cm
   5. 18 sq cm

Exercises 9.4

1. a. C
   i. CA, CB, CD ii. PQ iii. AD
   b. O
   i. OP, OS ii. PQ iii. QR
4. a. 20 cm b. 12 cm c. 34 cm d. 200 cm

5. a. 8 cm b. 11 cm c. 25 cm d. 4 cm

6. $\frac{1}{2}$ m = 50 cm

7. F, 6 cm

CHAPTER 10

Exercises 10.1

1. a. X b. ✓ c. ✓ d. ✓ e. X
2. a. Y b. N c. N d. N
4. a. Y b. Y c. N

CHAPTER 11

Exercises 11.1

1. a. 2, 1

   b. 200, 200, 200, 200, 200

   c. 1, 1

   d. 1, 500, 500

Exercises 11.2

1. 5
2. a. 2 b. 4 c. 5 d. 3
3. a. 2500 b. 250 c. 1500 d. 500 e. 3000

Exercises 11.3

1. 2 kg 500 g
2. 37 kg 775 g

Exercises 11.4

1. a. 10000 ml b. 14000 ml c. 25250 ml d. 5990 ml
2. a. 8 1 b. 3, 805 c. 26, 420 d. 4, 875
3. 16
4. 1 1

Measurement of length

1. 1000 2. 400 3. 720 4. 6105 5. 3, 500
6. 6 7. 1 8. 8, 26

Exercises 11.5

1. a. 243 m 20 cm   b. 223 km 151 m   c. 157m 34 cm

2. a. 251 km 957 m   b. 328 m 23 cm   c. 26 m 19 cm

3. 25 m 90 cm

4. 101 km 952 m

Measurement

1. a. ml   b. ml   c. l   d. m   e. cm
   f. g   g. g   h. km

2. a. 500   b. 600   c. 60   d. 700

CHAPTER 12

Exercises 12.1

1. a. 2:45, Quarter to 3   b. 12:45, Quarter to 1
   c. 6:50, 10 mins to 7

2. a. 3:55, 5 mins to 4   b. 5:45, Quarter to 6
   c. 8:55, 5 mins to 9   d. 9:50, 10 mins to 10

Exercises 12.2

1. a.m., a.m., p.m., p.m.

2. a. 11.40 a.m   b. 5.20 p.m   c. a.m   d. p.m
   e. p.m   f. p.m   g. p.m   h. p.m
   i. midnight   j. p.m   k. a.m   l. p.m

Exercises 12.3

1. a. 1630 hrs b. 2345 hrs c. 1815 hrs d. 1053 hrs
   e. 2045 hrs f. 0950 hrs g. 0000 hrs h. 1610 hrs
   i. 0755 hrs j. 1735 hrs

2. a. 12.30 a.m. b. 10.05 p.m. c. 9.40 a.m. d. 9.10 p.m.
   e. 5 p.m. f. 1.15 g. 1 a.m. h. 8.50 p.m.

Exercises 12.4

1. a. 3h 40 m b. 7 h 55 m c. 11 h 50 m d. 7 h 50 m
   e. 14 h 25 m f. 14 h 25 m g. 12 h
2. a. 11.50 a.m. b. 4 a.m. c. 9 a.m. d. 12.55 a.m.
   e. 5.50 p.m.
3. a. 5.05 b. 9.40 c. 4.30

4. a. 9.25 p.m. b. 12.40 p.m. c. 6, 45 d. 1.15 p.m.

Exercises 12.5

1. a. 33 b. 52
2. 44
3. 15 Oct
4. 20 Dec

CHAPTER 13

Exercises 13.1

1. a. ₹ 997.45 b. ₹ 583.20
2. ₹ 204.15

3. ₹ 197.65

Exercises 13.2

1. a. ₹ 1890 b. ₹ 854
2. a. ₹ 701 b. ₹ 681
3. 260, ₹ 6
4. ₹ 311

Mental Maths

1. a. ₹ 600 b. ₹ 70 c. ₹ 2.65
2. (246.60 + 64.40)

3. ₹ 65

CHAPTER 14

Exercises 14.1

1. a. 63, 83, 103, 123 b. 188, 186, 184, 182
   c. D1, E2, F1, G2 d. TS, RQ, PO, NM
   e. 1990, 1980, 1970, 1960

2.

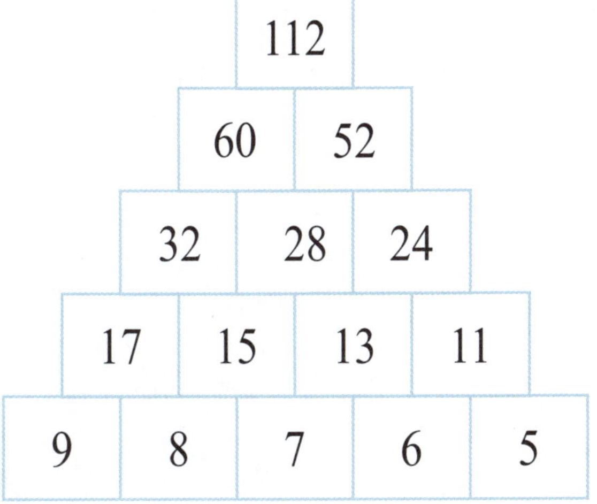

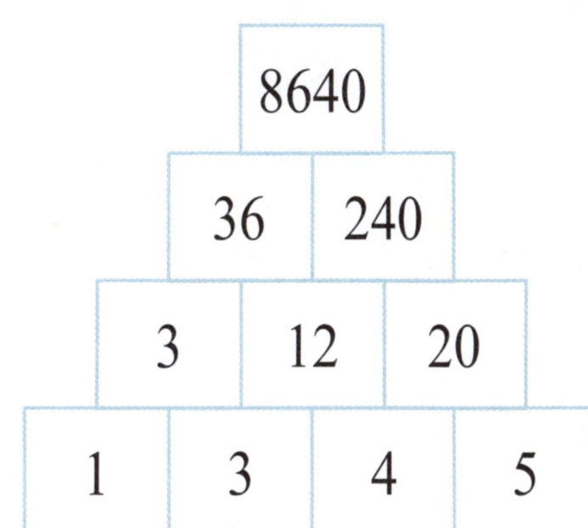

3. a. I am an Indian.
   b. Gandhi ji is my hero.
   c. I love cricket.

4. a. 25 16120951420
   b. 25 8151452120
   c. 14522517 1295

CHAPTER 15

Exercises 15.1

1. Refer to fig. 2 on pg 134
   a. Cricket b. 3 c. 3 d. 43

3. a. Rimi b. Rani, Mini c. 4 d. Rekha

4. a. 25 b. Orange c. Mango, Apple d. Pear

Review Exercise 1

1. a. 100000 b. 100, 10 c. 1 lakh d. 86999
   e. 1977 f. 500 g. 4,68,001 h. 100000, 3, 0, 0, 4, 1
   i. 70,000 j. 3300

2. a. Six lakh fifty thousand three, Six hundred fifty thousand three
   b. Three lakh ninty thousand five hundred, Three hundred ninty thousand and five hundred

3. a. 400010 b. 530,000

5. 1,04,698

6. a. xviii b. xxx c. X d. –

8. 99,999

9. 137

10. 74263

11. a. 29,421 b. 10001 c. 69,020 d. 92,888 e. 100000

Review Exercise 2

1. a. 6000, 1200

2. 7020 a. 320 b. 82

4. a. 2360 b. 1840 c. 3077, sum 7277

5. 2280

6. 7914

7. 24 h 40 mins

8. 6 h 45 mins

9. 3.40 p.m.

10. 15

Review Exercise 3

1. a. 2976 b. 8808 c. 21072 d. 94341 e. 241120
   f. 163440 g. 6232 h. 83996 i. 190232

2. 5069; 9650

3. 341250

4. 161
5. 7935

6. 64, 60

7. 58; 6

8. 9.15 a.m.

Review Exercise 4

1. 21, 909

2. 9001

3. 2, 42, 570

4. 63, 442

5. 47789

6. 6a

7. 62, 012

8. 26, 678

9. a. 14000 b. 28000 c. 73000 d. 5000

Review Exercise 5

1. a. 543, 15 b. 102, 16 c. 172, 40 d. 466, 16 e. 159, 8
   f. 182, 29 g. 395, 4 h. 153, 14 i. 82, 20 j. 479, 10
2. 64
3. 141
4. 230
5. 642
6. 3
7. a. $\frac{6}{14}, \frac{18}{42}, \frac{30}{70},$ b. $\frac{10}{40}, \frac{8}{32}, \frac{5}{20}$ c. $\frac{4}{10}, \frac{6}{15}, \frac{8}{20}$

Review Exercise 6

1. a. 45 km 425 m b. 39 kg 930 g c. 69 l 606 ml
2. a. 12 l 475 ml b. 2 kg 350 g
3. 6 l 750 ml
4. ₹ 35000
5. ₹ 1585
6. 5
7. 257